PERSPECTIVES

STORY & MEMOIR

Praise for Other Titles by this Author

A BREAK IN THE CHAIN

'A bold and imaginative re-writing of Tansley's famous family's history, told with the dedication of the historian and the imaginative flair of the novelist … She transforms the veiled landscape of the past into an enthralling panoply which speaks to her readers in the present. A well-written and gripping book and far more than the story of a migrant family.'

Novelist, columnist and literary critic Alan Gold

'This is a warm, lively, empathetic novel full of fascinating social history.'

Sydney Morning Herald

'This has movie written all over it.'

Denis Walter, *3AW, Sydney*

'Tansley brings alive her father's stories of the development of Melbourne. The blend of fact and fiction gives this book its richness.'

writingWA

'A beautifully written imagining of three generations of her family.'

Herald Sun

'At the core of the book is Judaism and what it means when affection strays beyond religious barriers. Tansley records the lives of her ancestors not in an imaginative, fictive construct. She has a lot of spaces in the record to fill and her responses are largely pitch perfect.'

The Sunday Age

'An engaging story that gives a human face to Melbourne's explosive growth during the gold rush … This book will resonate with anyone who has ever witnessed the deep, astonishing antagonism to an interfaith relationship, and the permanent damage to family ties that such antagonism can cause.'

Bracha Rafael, *Galus Australis*

'Richly researched, splendidly illuminating. *A Break in the Chain* offers insider history, the private story beyond the public history, an emotionally dense and intriguing Australian story of high achievement, and of cultures and traditions in rich conflict.'

Writer and academic Michael Meehan

FOR WOMEN WHO GRIEVE

'Our culture, by and large, is not comfortable with this kind of reality: we prefer not to think about death, loss or loneliness. That is why this book is important, and for all of us – not just to those who have recently lost a partner. Loss is not the opposite of gain in terms of our deepest humanity. It can be its other side, if we know how to live it through.'

The late Veronica Brady
Member of the Loreto order of Roman Catholic nuns

'Tansley's warm personal disclosures will undoubtedly assist women who mourn; those who feel lost and dejected will find joy and hope in place of despair, and a sense of purpose for the future.'

Canberra Times

'The clear message from one grieving woman to others is that "you are not alone" and that your experience is valued and normal.'

Australian Health Review

'An essential and valuable addition to any collection of "help" books on the painful and sensitive subject of death, dying, and the process of grieving.'

Midwest Book Review

'This book is written in the form of a series of steps to take the reader gently through different stages of grief: understanding death, letting go, being gentle with yourself, world of words, dreaming, mind control …'

Weekly Times (Vic)

National Library of Australia Cataloguing-in-Publication data
Tansley, Tangea – author.
Perspectives: Story and Memoir/Tangea Tansley.
978-0-9941625-4-0 (paperback)
Tansley, Tangea. Author, Australian. Short stories. Memoir. Fiction, memoir, biography.

Epigraph: Thelma Thompson quoting her father in Dale Carnegie, *How to Stop Worrying and Start Living*, Chaucer Press, Suffolk, p. 178.

Cover design by Su Halfwerk/Novel Prevue
Cover image by Viv Tansley

TANGEA TANSLEY was born in what is now Zimbabwe and lived and worked in many countries around the world before settling in Perth, Western Australia. She published her first short story "The Kookaburra's Laugh" when she was twenty-one and other short stories and essays have been published, broadcast and have received awards in national competitions. She is the author of three novels and several books of non-fiction. *Perspectives: Story & Memoir* is her first collection of short stories and memoir. She has a website and occasional blog at www.tangeatansley.com.

ALSO BY TANGEA TANSLEY

NOVELS

A Break in the Chain: the Early Kozminskys

Out of Place

A Question of Belonging

NON-FICTION

For Women Who Grieve

Heytesbury Stud

Our Grand Design

PERSPECTIVES

STORY & MEMOIR

TANGEA TANSLEY

Two men looked out from prison bars
One saw the mud, the other saw stars

Thelma Thompson

CONTENTS

INTRODUCTION

'Life is a series of beginnings and endings,' my Aunt Nan once said to me as we sat on the steps of the caravan she shared with her forty-three cats. It was a fine day in county Sussex some thirty or so years ago and I can remember the saying as quite new to me back then. It was delivered so crisply that the words fell about my ears like autumn leaves and I've had cause to remember them on many an occasion since.

Beginnings and endings and, in between, a story. Birth and death and, in between the two events, a journey. Inseparable from both creation and finale, it is the 'in-between' that is the stuff of our human condition and of the books and stories we read and write. *The Journey, not the Arrival, Matters* was both the theme and title of the last volume of Leonard Woolf's autobiography – and it is *journey* that drives this collection of story and memoir.

In the Story section of *Perspectives*, I've tried to capture this interstitial space from the viewpoints of a range of characters, both human and animal. For the most part, the players are ordinary folks trying to make sense of the cards they've been dealt and the choices they've made as they struggle with the reality of being human in a not-always-humane world. **Bitsa** tells the story of a boy and the dog that adopts him which sets off a chain of consequences that neither could have predicted; in **Middle Man**, the lonely protagonist loses a friend only to find a new way of moving forward; **My Mother Was a Russian Spy** foretells the possibility of change for a rather lost young woman.

The Memoir component of the book tells stories that are closer to home – at times, slices of perplexing circumstance that have accompanied my own journey, or events taken from the lives of people who have touched my life and, in doing so, left an indelible thumbprint.

To end this collection, I have taken the unusual step of including a story by my late father, Ken Coton. See Postscript for more about Dad and his story **Then Came Fury**.

A number of the pieces have been published previously. In these cases, I have tended to keep the style of dialogue used by the first published source although at times this deviates from the norm of the collection.

STORY

THE GAMBLER

In my driving mirror, the road behind me rears up and tumbles from view like the caterpillars of grey felt that wheeled out from under the foot of my mother's sewing machine in another lifetime. I've lost count of the number of times I've travelled this highway, but it was at least once a year until she died. And then, after that, I went north every few months until it was clear they were coping fine, my sister Susie and Dad.

The slip of peach-pale paper on the dashboard is reflected in the sloping glass of the windscreen; the image bobs in front of my eyes until I move it away. And then back again. Any small thing to keep awake.

Although, in actual fact, the lottery ticket is not a small thing, no small thing at all. It's the one thing I buy without fail each Monday and post straightaway to *Jingaree* so Dad gets it in time for the weekend. In the beginning, I did it as much for myself as for him. In a way it balanced out the guilt of not being there, this small gift that had built into it such a raft of possibilities. It was something, too, that I had to remember to do myself. To go to the newsagent, circle the numbers, slip the ticket into one of the envelopes I kept in a corner of the glove box. I'd tried to get him to join a syndicate. Much more chance, I'd said. More reliable, too. But I lacked the persuasive capabilities of our mother and even on the end of the line all those miles to the north, I could feel his resistance, see his slippers digging into the carpet. Nothing would satisfy him but that I choose the numbers myself, so long as there was at least one in the thirties among them. And him not a betting man. Or was he? He'd married our mother, hadn't he?

They'd come out from England with a bit of money longer ago than I liked to remember. Our mother had hated the young city with Dad getting up each morning to put on a clean shirt and his only suit to go out looking for work. She fretted, waiting, knowing the news when he came back would be the same as yesterday and the day before and you could see the fear growing in her that their savings would trickle away, bit by bit, every penny of it spent on hope. Somehow Perth failed her from the start and, though she never said how or why, you could tell.

Then, one day, she had her idea.

'Let's go north,' she said, the words out of her mouth before he was barely in the door, before he'd had a chance to take off his jacket and loosen his tie. And then she said it again, just as if she'd never said it before, as he threw himself in an armchair and she put a cup of strong sweet tea in his hands. 'Let's go up north,' she said that day as if the idea had blown in the door along with the hot wind from the east.

'Go north,' he repeated, still thinking perhaps of the bus driver who had sailed on by, pretending not to notice him standing at the stop. 'Go up north?'

'Yes,' she nodded. 'Buy a station, like. A cattle station.' Her eyes glowed. She was a pretty woman and when her eyes sparkled like that he would have given her anything she asked for, even a cattle station; he'd have figured out some way. But he was still back there at the bus stop and hadn't had the long day to think it through as she had. So he just stared back at her, confused, and a bit cross to cover the confusion.

'Why not?' She was sitting forward in her chair and you could tell from the knit of her fingers that it wasn't until this moment of telling him that the idea to her became real, less wild, something that could actually be achieved. 'Just imagine, the splendid isolation of it, William.

All lovely and warm all through the year and we could grow all our own food. Heh?'

He could be forgiven for being less than enthusiastic; his work as a sales rep hardly lent itself to farming savvy, let alone on the scale of a station. But as I've said, she was a persuasive woman, my mother, and once she'd set her mind, determined. The alternative, she said, was opal-mining in Andamooka which, come to think of it, would be an adventure as well as more lucrative, where they could live in a cave and make their fortune. You could see him start to fidget as she outlined this second plan, fearing that it would take precedence over the first and seeing himself even less of a miner than a cattle station owner. And that was really all it took.

Although what they bought wasn't exactly a cattle station, hardly a farm really, being the awkward bin-end of a huge property. But it was large enough to run a small herd of cattle and had isolation enough to satisfy the fussiest hermit. But it was the house that captured our mother's imagination, fulfilling her expectations of Australia in a way the city had failed to do. We knew from the moment she saw it that we would be moving north.

'It's a homestead,' she said, turning to our father, her eyes brimming. She put her hand on his arm, gently and in great wonder, and it was exactly as if he'd built it himself just for her. 'A real homestead, Will.' And in fact she was right. It was a dinkum Aussie farmhouse with the driveway sweeping around in front of the steps, a wisp of a vine to lend it some green, wide shady verandahs and a tin roof. 'Twin chimneys,' she murmured.

As for Dad – if Mum was happy, so was he, although it was clear from the first that he wasn't a beef farmer. Three times in all the big trucks arrived to collect the cattle, but by the third year they'd all gained personalities and names – or names and personalities – and it was hard for him that year. He watched the red dust toss up behind the truck as it disappeared on its way back to the highway and he watched every fleck of it fall back down to the ground again. And then he disappeared into the big shed at the back of the farmhouse and next thing we knew there was a roaring and smashing that went on so long that the three of us stood not breathing, statues in O'Grady's game. It was my little sister, finally, who asked should we go and see.

'No,' our mother had said. 'Just let him be.' But we all knew what had upset him, and that was the last time the cattle were collected for slaughter. It is the only time I remember seeing my father lose his temper.

As I draw up in a small swish of gravel, my sister is there to greet me, already down the steps and hugging me with Dad not far behind, stepping down one foot at a time, his cane tap-tapping ahead of him.

'Why don't you put your stuff straight in your room?' Susie says. 'There's a cuppa ready and waiting. You must be parched.' The fair hair I've always envied is paler than ever against the warm tan of her face, but there's a web of white around her eyes I haven't noticed before and she's leaner than I remember.

'Ah, how nice this is,' our father says once we're all settled. 'My two daughters.' He raises his cup and leans into his comfy chair. 'To my two daughters,' he says again. His face beams out of the dark cool of the room. He couldn't be happier, I realise. All my worries over the years thickly threaded with guilt, afraid that we hadn't been stern enough with him when our mother died, that we should have been firmer about his leaving the farm, all quite unnecessary. I smile back about to take a sip of my own tea when all of a sudden he sits upright.

'Did you bring it?'

I'm about to ask, quite automatically and stupidly, 'Bring it? Bring what?' when I remember. The ticket, of course, still on the dash.

'Oops. Still in the car. Just a jiff.' I'm up and out of the chair.

'No hurry,' he calls after me. But of course there is; there is a need for hurry. I can tell that from the way he crosses and uncrosses his legs.

When I give it to him, he takes it in both hands. All his life he had been aiming to make his fortune. Now here it is, contained in the infinite possibility of this slim piece of paper.

'Ah, yes, this is it.' His voice is gruff, his face alight, his mouth moving along with his eyes, as if he's tasting the numbers as he reads. 'A good sequence. Two thirties. This is the one. Thank you, Melissa. Ah, yes, yes.'

Still holding the token in both hands, he kisses it, raises it above his head. I glance at my sister, but Susie is reading, quite unmoved, and it occurs to me it's quite possible he does this every week. The money is going to help us all, of that he's convinced. A new car for Susie; that always tops the list. 'Something big,' he'd say. 'Keep her safe. You need that on these roads.' After that, the list of items was no less important, but quite vague. Like improvements to the farm. 'Bring it up to date a bit. Not much's been done to it since your mother's time.' Small things, too, that obviously bother him, like the dripping tap in his bathroom. It was going to fix everything, this Lotto win. But even the waiting for it helped because if there was something he needed, he'd just shrug, 'All well, we'll just have to wait until the money comes in.'

Standing next morning on the iron-grey boards of the verandah, it occurs to me how different the property looks from this perspective. Coming in, I'd been faced with the grand gates beyond which the pretty homestead was as welcoming as ever, but looking back the other way, it's not difficult to see how it would be improved by having money spent on it. In fact, as I look, really look, I see things I haven't noticed before. Or is it just that I'm seeing for the first time? Because fencing doesn't deteriorate quite so quickly, at least not fall down as it's doing in the paddock right ahead of me. Does it?

I walk down the steps and out onto the property and everywhere I go it's the same, the state of the farm coming into focus like a photograph in an acid bath. Hay bales not properly covered, gone sour and left to rot, the tin roofs of the sheds well-peppered with holes so the sun trickles in, and from the look of the machinery, the rain too; the tractor our father had been so proud of is starting to rust and looks as though it hasn't been used in years. There's a small vegetable plot that is well-tended, mulched thickly with the mouldy hay. And chickens scratching about in the dust. I bend to pick up an egg from under a bush, start when Susie comes up behind me, her boots soundless in the dust. My face is suddenly hot.

'Dad looks incredibly happy,' I say quickly. 'You're doing a fabulous job with him, Susie. I haven't seen him so sprightly in years.' And then when Susie doesn't respond, I look down at the egg in my hands, pass it to her. 'Here. Found this … under that bush.'

She puts out her hand, takes it slowly.

'No knowing how long that's been there. I'll have to test it.'

'You don't keep the chooks in the run anymore?'

'No,' she shrugs. 'It's just one more thing to do, isn't it? Put them away at night, let them out in the morning. They're happier this way anyway.' She looked off into the distance.

'Look? Is something the matter?'

She swings back to face me.

'I don't want to do this anymore, Lissa.'

'Don't want to do *what* anymore? The farm?'

'The farm. Dad. The whole bang shoot.'

'But Dad's so happy.' The words are out too quickly. My sister's eyes flash and for a moment it's my mother here in front of me.

'Yes. Dad's happy. So long as he gets his meals, his cups of tea and his bloody ticket each week, Dad's happy. Why wouldn't he be?'

'But. But you. You love it here.'

'Do I?' Her voice is ferocious. 'Do I? I'm not so sure I do anymore. If he ever wins that lottery …' She gives a short laugh, turns and stalks back to the house.

It's getting dark when Susie switches on the box, the three of us sitting around the machine as if it's the god of all things good. Which, for these precious moments, I suppose it is.

Extracting the slip from his top pocket, Dad places it on the small table in front of him, together with his pen and a notebook. The screen is directly in front of him and it's difficult to tell who's watching it more intently, my father or my sister. Even in the darkened room, I can see the colour in his face is high, almost as if he has a fever. Susie's thin face shines white.

'These wretched ads,' he mutters. His feet twitch. But then it's there. The presenter in her sequinned gown, the six white balls twirling. The next moments may change the rest of our lives. He rubs his hands, sits forward in his chair, picks up the pen.

'There she blows,' he cries. 'Thirty!' I can see he wants to jump up, shake my hand, but equally that he's loath to take his eyes from the screen. The next thirty seconds are tense enough, but recording the numbers is only the first part. Now he has to go through each of the ten rows, checking and double-checking and then, I suspect, Susie will do her own check. Just in case. My sister slips out of the room while I continue to watch my father sitting in the noisy half-dark, oblivious to everything but the figures before him, his tongue resting on his lips as he squeezes the numbers dry.

But like most times, at the end of it, there's nothing to be won. Nothing at all.

'You check,' he says, half-rising to pass it across. 'Just in case.' And I feel as if he's passed across a load of responsibility as heavy as a concrete truck, as if I alone can change the luck that has skirted so carefully around him all his life.

As I bend over the column of figures, I can feel the hope run out of him. His shoulders sag.

'Don't worry,' he says finally. 'It's not your fault.'

'*What's* not my fault?'

'Oh, you know, the money. Me winning or not winning. You keep sending them up, these tickets, and I know you do it for the best, dear. I know you do it for the best. Every week, you send me a ticket and it's good of you to take the trouble.

'But as to winning. I'm not sure it's right. I'm not sure whether winning is the right thing for me.' He looks down at his hands, rests the tips of his fingers together and his voice is low, almost a mumble, and so I'm not sure whether he's talking to me or to himself.

'You see, it would change things … change everything, if ever one of those tickets came in a winner.' He raises one eyebrow, jerks his chin towards the kitchen where Susie is preparing tea. And then his eyes look into mine. 'And, you see, Melissa, I don't think I could bear that.'

'You mean, you know that – you know how it would change things – and yet each week?'

'Each week.' He nods slowly, his face flashing from red to green to yellow and back again as the machine flickers in the half-dark.

In losing, each week he wins. And all these years I'd thought him down on his luck.

A QUESTION OF TIME

I'm in a chair in a room I've never seen before. I grip at the armrest, breathe, shake my head and blink until the jangling in my head gives way to a different sound – to a whirring and pounding like a mob of kangaroos on the march.

Women, mostly women, passing by the open door of this too-square room in clumps of twos and threes, some with sticks, others struggling with steel contraptions obstinate as shopping trolleys. A wheelchair on the outside, another flashing past. Such concentration and determination might indicate a fire, in which case shouldn't I be joining the throng instead of sticking to the plastic seat of this chair? This is absurd.

As I start to rise two men in orange overalls wheel in a flat-bed trolley. But they're moving like men obeying a go-slow, so it is unlikely to be a fire. As they pass in front of me, within a metre of my feet, it occurs to me to wonder whether in fact I'm here at all or whether this is part of a dream and I'll wake up to find myself writing away at my desk.

I go through the breathe-and-blink routine again. Can see enough to look around. The men are over by a window that looks out onto a sort of concrete courtyard. Closer to me – within reach – is another trolley, three tiers of shiny metal that make me think syringes, cotton wool, kidney-shaped bowls. Except this one holds something of a jumble. On the top shelf, a hairbrush, a comb and a silver-backed mirror, a small china trinket box with a crack in one side, an unopened bottle of Coco Chanel. On the middle shelf a stack of books and on the lowest a collection of pantsuits, pilling jumpers and blouses. I start to reach out towards the books, diaries with covers all the colours of Joseph's coat, and then I pull back. My hands press into the damp wood of the chair arms. Any minute I can get up and go.

The men finish what they are doing, wipe their hands on the sides of their grubby workwear and walk out. A slice of sunlight cuts the room in half, bounces off the trolley. I concentrate on the sunlight and then the little china box painted with the scene of a battle. Look at it, look more closely, I order myself. Pick it up and bring it to your face; hold it so you can see quite clearly it is St. George who isn't a saint at this point in his own story, but someone who is brave and skilled enough to kill a dragon. His red-and-white shield protects his chest; in his right hand he holds an advisedly lengthy lance destined to pin the unfortunate dragon to the English soil. It was that lance and the way he used it that brought George to the attention of the Church who commissioned all the artists in the land to paint a fair likeness of the scene so the unruly populace would realise just how expertise with the lance combined with a bit of derring-do could benefit a person and give them something to aim for. It got George the princess, too, now I come to think of it, which was probably more up his alley at the time than thoughts of ending up on a trinket box. Handy weapon a lance. Lances come in different guises.

Any minute I can get up and go. That I know. Knowing is a type of lance. *Knowledge is power*, I remember saying to the children one lunchtime, at which they raised their eyes from their plates for long enough to nod at me before looking up at the ceiling. The men return, each with a carton hugged to his chest, the older of the two quite red in the face. Choosing not to see me. Or perhaps they can't? Perhaps I'm a ghost. The graduate. Behind plate-glass of unimaginable thickness, banned from the church, barred from communicating, expelled from school, freed from life's lessons, pounding, screaming, desperate to be heard. Behind plate-glass. I know plate-glass. When my husband died and I was still on my knees begging him to stay, I could see him hovering above, you know, unable to pull me to my feet, to tell me that everything would be all right – that one day, it would be all right – which, in the end, of course, it was. With one small catch: it wasn't yet the end.

They set down the boxes and leave again; the stack in the far corner rises. What do they contain and why are they here? For that matter, why am *I* here amid this growing pile of cartons? I try to rise, but there's a message not happening between my brain and my legs.

Concentrate. This chair is wet and the trinket box belongs to the other woman. The diaries belong to the other woman. This room belongs to the other woman. But then there are other things. Like the dressing table that arrives next to be hefted in by the two chaps who look as if they hate it already, hate it as much as I do. Which makes me wonder why I hung onto it so long. Too heavy and red and all-round difficult entirely. Lacking in all subtlety and style. Never liked jarrah, anyway. They set it down with a bump in a corner of the nursery-blue room where it crouches uncertainly – as out of place as a cockroach on Howard Hughes' dinner table.

And then, quite randomly it seems to me – or perhaps it's the sudden noise of it that startles me – someone tears at the flap of one of the cartons. Starts to unpack. Right in front of me. Framed photos, the clock that has always contorted each second with a loud and measured click like a dripping tap. A nightmare – except the sweaty plastic I'm sitting on suggests it isn't.

Under cover of the rush and rustle of paper, I whisper to check the working of my voice, wave my hand at the young lass kneeling behind the pile of unravelling newspaper.

'What are you doing? Why am I here?'

She starts as if she'd thought herself alone. And then closes her mouth which is a pity because it's somewhat determined, as such mouths are. No, not so much determined as bored.

'The matron shouldn't be too long. I wouldn't think.'

'Matron? What matron?'

She shrugs. 'She'll talk to you.'

'Talk to me? What about? Meanwhile I don't want any of this. Please arrange for it to be returned to my home.'

She doesn't stop what she's doing, but her eyelids flicker, she glances at me briefly. 'But you will, you know. You'll find you need your stuff. When you settle in, you'll find it's all a great comfort to you. Just you wait and see.'

My glance strays from the dressing table to the pile of belongings mounting in front of us. 'I'd like to see the matron. Or whoever's in charge. Now.'

I'd like to think my voice is firm, but I suspect she hears something I don't. Her lips tighten just a smidgen more and in a trice she's on her feet and out the room. For some reason, as she leaves, I find myself reaching again for the stack of diaries. This time, scooping them up as if they're Belgian chocolates, I stash them away at the rear of the deep bedside locker, close the door as the matron arrives – a tall thin woman whose deep frown suggests she's having the bad day she had been expecting all along.

'What's all this?' She stops in the act of rubbing her hands together. 'Oh dear. You shouldn't have been brought in here until all this …' The crease between her eyebrows deepens. 'Until your room was ready. I'm really sorry.'

There's a silence while I absorb the right of possession I have just been granted. *My* room. Have I bought it? Or just rented it for the duration? Am I ill? Perhaps I fell and hit my head? Or has time marched on without my knowing? I've always been too busy living to pay much attention to things like the passing of time.

'That's not the point. I need some sort of explanation for what's going on. Why am I here? How did I get here?' From the indignity of my pale plastic throne I wave my hand at the room. 'And what on earth is all this doing here?'

She straightens her back. 'You don't think you need it now, but you will. I can assure you that once you settle in …'

Settle in? In the split second before my brain flames and my eyes glow red, I turn the phrase over in my mind.

She goes to step into the gap. 'I don't think you …' she starts, and then stops. For a moment she looks as trapped as me. We look at each other, two animals calculating the odds in this small space with nowhere to go.

I shrink from her as she stretches out her hand to touch me on the shoulder; she crouches down in front of me instead. 'A little later we'll have a good talk. But now is not the time. Meanwhile, how about I get all the boxes removed and we can store your things in the back room for a short while? Precious stuff, these memories.'

It's only when I drop back into the chair that I realise I had half-risen. No place to go but my own body.

'What about this on the trolley? Don't you want that either?' Her voice is gentle.

'No,' I say. 'That's not mine.'

'Not yours. You mean?' Shakes her head. 'This is bad.' Sighing, she grasps the handle of the trolley and steers the remaining bibs and bobs of the other woman to their resting place. If she were Indian, that woman, and she'd outlived her husband, her belongings would have been burned along with her body. Me, too. I'd no longer be here. Can't help thinking they got it right, the Hindus. All these widowy widows hobbling about the corridors.

'Not everything of you will be trashed,' I promise the pale face that floats in and out the shadows about my bed that first night. 'They can't take your memories. They can't take *all* your story.' It is a small enough rebellion, but it lightens just a little the gloom of that solid darkness.

When I think about it, which is often, events divide into before and after. In fact it's the only date that comes to mind, that Friday 13th he dropped neatly dead at my feet and divided my life in two.

'Are you sad?'

I open my eyes, lower my lids against the glare of the falling sun. A young child, maybe seven or eight, is sitting on the low wall of a round structure which I can only think is meant to resemble a well. A wishing well in the centre of the concrete courtyard. At the bottom of which must live Mimir, god of wisdom. If Odin sacrificed his eye to Mimir for the knowledge of why things are the way they are, what would I sacrifice? And do I have anything left to sacrifice that can help me now? I shake my head to round up the thought-lines that show a new tendency to trot off down random laneways like sheep in search of their Bo Peep.

'Why? Why are you so sad?' she asks again.

A girl-Fauntleroy with copper curls, her lips slightly apart. A Rubens. Renoir. Or, closer in time and place, a Florence Rodway pastel, with her gift for capturing the likenesses of children as children. She is painterly, this kid. *I* could paint her. I *could have* painted her. Beauty and ugliness are easy to capture. It's the stuff in between there's no name for. Or is it that the stuff in between is not worth recording? It's not always a matter of perspective. No. Not. Definitely not, because perspective is itself an unstable term. Keats got it half-right. Something of beauty is easy to identify and, for its duration, gives effortlessly and unthinkingly its full measure of pleasure. It's with the forever bit that he went wrong.

'I'm not sad.'

'Well. You *look* sad.'

'Well, I'm not.' I wonder whether she is aware that she is sitting on the edge of a wishing well? Do they teach children about such things these days? Sunday lunch and the wishbone. Close your eyes and wish on the breastbone of a dead bird. Wishes come true, so long as you don't cheat. Blue eyes, of course, to go with the red-gold hair. God must have been thoroughly bored with his own image by the time he finished with humans. Didn't really exercise his right brain until he started on dogs. Although I read somewhere recently that the left-brain-right-brain theory has gone the way of the wishbone and the wishing well.

But what if I tell the truth? That I'm so sad I'm a cracked pot or a bucket without a bottom, so everything you put in falls straight through? That I can't open my eyes any further because the sun's so low it looks right in? But that regardless of whether my eyes are open or closed, I can see her anyway because she reminds me of a little girl I once knew? Have I forgotten how to be real?

'Are you my daughter?'

She stares. Something in her look reminds me of the tooth under the pillow that the mouse was going to replace with a coin. And didn't because it forgot, so when the scrap of ivory with its new pink-red disconnection was still there in the toe of the pink slipper in the morning, the child of long ago looked just like the statue in front of me, her mouth slightly open, a slight frown of confusion, trembling sad.

I tighten the skin around my eyes to deepen the blackness, but she's left her imprint on the inside of my lids. And in here, in the dark of where I spend much of my time, it's not clear to me which part of the girl lingers. Her face or the yellow-and-white sundress with the bright pink roses around the hem? A moment captured. Paint. Photo. Memory. Belief. Disbelief. You are what you believe. Or somewhere in between. It doesn't matter. Or later. *You can't cope*. Nonsense, of course I can. *You'll leave something on. The kettle. It'll burn the house down.* Rubbish. It turns itself off. Most times. *Or the stove. The gas. And you won't even know it's on. Please, please, don't be difficult.*

Difficult? Me? I always had a problem with the manipulation of logic.

'I'm here to see my grandma,' she volunteers.

You're in the right place, I think. There are a lot of grandmothers here. It's a sort of grand holding pen. The words are printed in my mind, but I don't think I speak aloud.

'Mum says she's lost the plot, my grandma.'

The plot? A selective choice. When there's so much else to lose from the story of a life.

'The plot?' I open my eyes, and my legs must have jerked out because the book spins off my lap. She's sitting just as she was before, one leg curled up, leaning back as if there's some sweet danger in toppling backwards into the unknown.

'Yes. Don't you know what that is?'

'No. No, I don't think I do. Tell me, I'm interested. What is *the plot* then?'

'Well.' Sits up a little straighter, smooths her skirt with hands that haven't yet lost their baby fat. Thank goodness she wears a skirt – though to my surprise it's not yellow-and-white with pink roses – and not the jumpsuit of the pink striped convict-variety the mothers favour these days. She's silent for a minute or two, nibbling at a nail and staring at her shadow twitching slightly on the ground front of her. I suspect the definition of plot has defeated her, but she's a winner with her next line. She has a future, this child.

'I think I have to go now.' She jumps down. 'Do you want your book back?' Without waiting for my answer, she picks it up, wipes her arm across the cover. 'That's funny writing!' She makes a face.

'It says "diary" in Arabic … in another language. It's a diary.'

'Is that what you read? Diaries are for *writing*, not reading.' But she looks uncertain as she hands the book back to me.

'It's a new habit of mine. A type of voyeurism. Or escapism.'

'I don't know what you mean.' She looks as me as if I'm demented.

'Voyeurism is like looking through a window. Into someone else's life. A rear window. And escapism, for me, is avoiding my own problems by becoming involved in someone else's. For me, in either case, it's a distraction.'

But she's bored suddenly with the game. Goes to skip off, looks back over her shoulder. 'I could come again. If you like? Next time. Do you want me to come again?'

Yes, yes. No, no. I close my eyes tight. But it's some time before I can shift her from the inside of my lids, sitting perched on the edge of a well of spent wishes with her leg crooked up and her cherry-pink panties on show.

Time – which should be precious, but somehow is not – is gobbled up by the bells that chime three times a day. Breakfast is a tray in bed. And crumbs. Lunch is a warm dish or sandwiches and tea or coffee. Tea is a similar warm dish. Sometimes there's soup. Mealtimes mark out the day and I find myself looking forward to them like an airline passenger fed up with making animal shapes out of cloud.

Now that I've got rid of the clock that ticked too loudly and my watch, the hands of which moved hardly at all, I rely on the bells. In fact, I play a game with the bells three times a day by planning to be somewhere between my chair and the door before the first chime rings out. Heads I win, tails the bells. And from the little piles of coins mounting on my bedside table, it looks as though I'll beat the bells by a small margin this week. My knuckles are white on the arm of the chair as I get ready to stand.

But then there's a tap on the inside of the part-open door and it's the flowers I see first. Sprigs of *Yesterday, today, and tomorrow.* My mother's favourite plant. She used to say it inspired her, though how she got inspiration from something fading – and thus terminal – beats me. A bunch of dark purple and mauve blossoms broken up by white. Dark green leaves. Birnam Wood, I think, as the short branch marches towards me, and then stops between me and my route to the door. With the bells about to ring at any moment. I hesitate half out of the chair.

'I wasn't quite sure whether you wanted to see me again,' she says, standing in front of me, holding out the sprays of drooping blooms. 'But I thought you'd like these. Purple, you see. My mother says purple colours are trendy at the moment. Like the binding on my dress.' One hand brushes at her dress. I take a breath. She's young. She doesn't know about the bells. About the game. Or about Father Time – that swindler who never gets it right, shelling out either too little or too much. And sure enough, the bells ring out.

Reading my face, she flushes. An uncomfortably large satchel sags from one of her shoulders and the hand holding the gift of purple wavers.

I try to rearrange my lips. I move a coin from one pile to the other, put the bells out of my mind. I go to rise to help her, but she lifts a hand.

'No. You don't have to get up. I can manage.' She hands the flowers to me while she unslings the satchel, lays it carefully in a corner of the room, advances towards the melamine cupboard under the vanity. 'Usually they keep the vases at the back,' she explains, her voice muffled. A moment later she emerges, her face even rosier, her hands empty. She glances quickly at the satchel and then around the room as if she hopes that by some stroke of good fortune a vase will pop up.

'Or this perhaps? This might do.' I hold out my water glass.

She skips across to me, the frown erased by her dimpled smile and we arrange the blooms together. We step back, heads on one side, to assess the effect of our handiwork.

'How did you find my room?'

'I asked them at the desk.'

'But you don't know my name.'

'I just said the person who reads a diary. And she said, Oh you must mean the one in Room 9.'

My name, title, gender swapped for a room with a number.

'How is your grandmother?'

But by now the corridor is on the move and I wonder whether she can hear me over the din. For a moment I think she is going to put her thumb in her mouth, instead she twists it into her skirt, shoots another glance into the corner of the room as if at any moment she might have to pick up her belongings and depart in a hurry. Which, indeed, she may.

'Do you still read your diary?'

'It's not actually mine.'

'Whose is it, then?'

'It belonged to a woman who is no longer here.'

'Did she let you read it? Isn't a diary only for the person who writes it? That's what my mother says.'

'Well, this woman didn't really have a choice. And, anyway, I'm not exactly scrupulous in that respect.'

Scrupulous may be beyond her, but she gets the gist the same moment she figures out where the other woman may have gone.

'You mean she …?'

I nod.

'Well,' she says tossing another glance at the satchel. 'Sometimes I think it's better to be dead than alive.' I raise my eyebrows. 'My grandma …' She picks at the amethyst hem of her white shift. 'I can hear she's breathing, but she's not *living*. Mum says *she's there on some level*. But I can't see what good that is. For her or us.' She breathes hard. 'When all we do is clean her up and turn her over and tuck her in so tight she can't move even if she could. And change the horrible green smelly flower water when she can't see the stupid flowers anyway.'

The crowd in the corridor has dissolved into the meal room. The room fills with her distress.

'Now *you* are the one who is sad,' I say. She takes one hand from her blotchy face.

'Why does it have to be like this? People getting old?'

I have no answer. I have no answer for myself. Let alone for a seven-year-old querying the meaning of existence.

'Here.' I move quickly to hand her the tissue box and as I do so something in the corner of the room catches my attention. The satchel moved. Or did it? Sometimes if my head swings too quickly, the rest of the room catches up. In slower motion.

Her eyes follow mine and she takes a deep shuddering breath. We both gaze at the satchel. Which twists a little, starts to shuffle across the floor towards us.

'Poor little thing.' She puts her head in her hands again. I move to the door, close it a little too sharply. Which halts the uneven march of the satchel and stops the child crying. Although it feels as though I've known her all my life, it occurs to me that I don't even know her name. It also occurs to me that it's probably time I took control.

'What's your name?'

'Vee.'

'Vee, what have you got in that bag?'

For an instant I think she's going to start wailing again, but she grabs a fistful of tissues instead.

'Something for you.'

'For me?' I glance down. So much for controlling the situation. The satchel is fairly moving now. Starts to jump and grumble until, with another look at me, she kneels to undo the straps.

Her eyes brim again as she draws forth a young puppy, way too young I would have thought to be away from its mother. Still kneeling she holds it to her as it burrows into her neck, releases its bladder. A fair amount of it for such a little pup. Dark yellow. Down the white dress with its trendy trim. Onto the floor. I watch the puddle widen; for the first time I thank the powers-that-be for linoleum.

'What is it?' I ask, meaning, of course, what breed. It's impossible to tell from either the length or colour of its coat, or its unformed features.

'I don't think it's any sort,' she says speaking into its coat. 'Just some beastly boys playing with it. They said they were going to drown it, that that's what happens to mongrels. So I gave them my pocket money. But then they …' She's squeezing the animal so hard, I have to suppress the thought that the drowning might have been a mercy. 'When I took it, him, home, my mother wouldn't let me keep him. She wants to send him to the pound. And it's so little …' Her voice ends on another wail.

I look towards the door.

'But what can I do? What do you want me to do? Talk to your mother?'

She dashes her face against her arm, snorts. 'She wouldn't be able to hear you. Once she's got something fixed in her mind, she can't hear anything.'

'Well.' I sit down. 'So how can I help?' I prompt. From the way the little chap is shivering, I wonder whether he'll see the day out.

She hugs the pup once more and then looks up at me. Her lips go to form a plea and my hand goes out to touch the soft fur.

The curtains are open to let in the winter sun and I'm sitting in my room looking out to the small courtyard with the wishing well in the middle. It is nearly time for the bells. Soon they will be here followed by the afternoon tea tray.

You might think I imagined all this? The little girl, the moving satchel and the puppy? Even I can't be very sure. When next I looked around the room, there was no little girl, no puppy and no puddle on the floor. The flowers were there, though, the trendy-coloured flowers resting their tired heads on the edge of what passes for a crystal vase.

My hand trembles as I select one of the diaries, the red one with the mildew on the back, and flip through the rather correct and timid writing to the entry of Saturday, July 7.

I am so so excited! Our second day at sea and tonight it's our turn to sit at the Captain's Table! Mother says she's going to check whether they have included me in the invitation. She says it's very unusual for anyone so young to be included although I don't count myself young at 17. So please God let it happen and if it does I'm going to wear my green chiffon. And, please, please, let me meet someone really really nice.

She did sit at the Captain's Table that night and she did wear the sea-green evening dress with the sequins at the waist. And, as it turned out, she did meet someone that very evening, someone who stayed with her for most of the rest of her life.

In fact, all the wishes she made that day came true. So tell me, Mimir, what would she wish for now? If she could have just one more wish?

GROWN MEN DON'T CRY

'And that's your last word, I take it. Ben.' But how is it that the question is not a question? How is it that Ben can think up a dozen ways he could have reframed his argument in the infinite pause between the end of the sentence and his name?

'I've got my – well – there's stuff I believe in.' His words are a mumble. He stares across the stacks of piled papers that run the length of his side of the wide desk, says more clearly. 'I can't do it.' When he should have said, *I'm afraid I can't do it*. Or *I can't do it, I'm afraid*. He should have shaken his head a little, looked down at his hands, bitten his bottom lip. Instead of, well, instead of looking as he did.

'Belief systems can be – expensive, Ben.' His boss runs his hand slowly over his hair: a buzz-cut as smooth as fresh-mown lawn. 'Well. Obviously, I can't persuade you. Collect your things and I'll arrange for pay in lieu. No need to stir things up.' When Ben fails to move, there's a degree of finality in his nod, and in the way he glances – almost casually – towards the door.

Fifteen years of shared deadlines shot through with shouts of sparkling triumph along with a fair number of ripped-up drawings and smashed keyboards are wrapped up in that nod. The desk widens until it's a forest of wood separating him from the other man who looks suddenly small and faraway. Or maybe it is he who is small and faraway? Soon you will be, Ben. Soon you will be. The important thing here is the distance that has opened quite suddenly between them. A chasm too wide to bridge. He pushes his trembling traitor hands deep into his pockets. So that's that then. In a sense, he had known it would happen sooner or later. The difference is that the 'sooner' has just arrived.

It makes it easier that everyone has left by the time he gets back to the Art department. In the recycling drawer in the tea room, he finds a bright yellow plastic bag, like a doggie-poo bag, but stronger, with a big happy smiling sun on one side. He doesn't feel like the smiling sun, he feels like shit as he sweeps his desk clear, upends drawers filled with brush pens and markers. To cheer himself up he could do one last drawing, a signature drawing. He's already swinging back to the drawing board, his fingers searching the bag for a pen, when he stops. Some things you do, some you don't. Want to show everyone you're not big enough to walk out of here without crying, Ben? What sort of a man are you? Even if there have been fifteen years of sharing that connect you to this desk and that board beside it. Even if there's only this half-filled bag to show for it. And a nod.

He turns on his heel to take a last look round, swings the sunny bag against his leg. He would whistle if he could. This is the time to whistle. For himself or for the watching walls. But he's never been much good at whistling.

From the bus stop, his home is a five-minute walk. That's not far, is it? Certainly not far enough right now. Home is Sue. Sue will have to be told. Or more precisely: *He* will have to tell Sue.

As he steps over the ridiculously low gate with the dodgy catch, she is right there, kneeling at the neatly scissored edge of her herbaceous border. Flowers bloom for Sue, herbs give off the sort of scent that makes you want to eat them chopped and sprinkled on a piece of buttered toast. Despite the mildness of the evening, her hat is pulled well over her nose, flowery gloves protect her hands, sleeves her arms. She's still wearing sunglasses; he wonders they don't damage her eyesight. Somewhere in among these layers of protection is his wife, but he knows who will have the most need of fortification over the next 45 seconds.

'I've been let go.' It sounds better than several alternatives he could have picked.

Still kneeling, leaning forward on her hands, she looks up at him through the narrow gap between sunglasses and hat.

'Hello Ben. Shall we start again? With something like: Lovely evening isn't it darling?' She pauses. '*Let go*? You mean: "made redundant"?'

'Well, not exactly.' He sucks at the insides of his cheeks. 'I resigned. Or maybe I was fired – I'm not exactly sure – because I refused to do the drawings for the new spray.'

'You what!' Still on her knees, she rears up like a caterpillar with a kitten's paw pinning its tail. 'You've done what?' Her voice suddenly very low as her gaze drops from his to the yellow bag.

'We've been over this before.' Which they had. Often. His inflexible determination that he will not be drawn into promoting products with which he doesn't agree. That's all there was to it really. Quite simple.

But Sue evidently doesn't think it simple. She drives the tines of the fork into the mushy earth and then she's on her feet, hands on hips, her earthy gloves digging into her crisp white shirt. He knows that stance.

'There's no bleeding of colour for you, is there? No wriggles or deviations in your straight lines? Your rights and wrongs are more regimented than the Chinese army. At your age, you've gone and walked out on one of the better-paid jobs in the art world. Just like that.' A soundless click in the air with her clumsy gloves, but she makes the point.

He shrugs. It's not the right time to explain that he didn't exactly walk out, that he'd be quite happy to be back where he was, that he'd thought the job would slide across to one of the others as it had in the past. And that he's as amazed as she that he's standing here with the happy bag drooping at his side. But on the plus side, he could point out that he also happens to be one of the most experienced, some might even say talented, graphic artists in the field, that he has an impressive portfolio and that he can't imagine that there'll be too much of a problem getting re-hired. It's been a long day.

'I'll put the tea on,' he says.

That night she packs the bag that has been packed and repacked more times than he can remember and goes to stay with her sister. Telling Sue had been bad. He had been right about that. But he is fairly certain that she will calm down just as quickly. Once she's been over his deficiencies a few times with her sister Babs, she'll start thinking of how much more understanding she could have been in the face of what, after all, rates as one of life's most stressful events.

He wakes to a morning filled with soft light, lies for a while with his hands clasped behind his head. Yesterday's defiance has softened and the other side of the bed looks, well, immeasurably spacious. But for now that's sort of okay.

He tries humming as he showers and shaves. He may not be able to whistle, but there is something nourishing in the sound waves of a hum. Since there is no knowing just when he may be called for an interview, he dresses in a pair of tan slacks and a white open-necked shirt instead of his usual jeans and T. And because he's in that sort of mood, he adds a rust-red scarf. You look a bit of a clown, Ben. But who cares?

Skipping breakfast, two minutes later he's on his mobile. He starts by calling his contacts. He drums his fingers on the kitchen counter while he waits for the receptionist to connect him. After the greetings, the point.

'It's like this, you see, Jim. I've just resigned from Mathieson's and wondered whether you might have a position I could fill? I've been with them for the last fifteen years, art director for the last ten. You've seen my work. I've –'

'Ben, Ben, stop. Before you go any further, mate, we're not looking for anyone right now. Sign of the times, you know. Besides we've got a good team together at present. But I'll certainly keep you in mind. And I'll ask around.

'Let me jot down a few details. Let's see. Fifteen years as department head, did you say?' Ben pictures him with his ballpoint hovering over a doodle pad. Was he an arrow man or a circle man?

'Ten years. I've –'

'Now if you were a web designer.'

'I –'

'And how old did you say you were – late forties?'

'Yes,' Ben lies.

By the end of the morning, he has made a dozen phone calls, dropped his age another couple of years. He wonders whether he's going about this the right way. Steady on, Ben, these things take time. You didn't expect them to be waiting for you, did you? Or did you? 'It's early days,' he says aloud. He makes himself a coffee, puts in two spoons of sugar instead of one, ditches it, starts again. When he drops the spoon in the sink, it sings like a metal dish dropped on tile. He sees himself reflected in the window of the oven as he passes, tugs off the scarf, drops it in the bin.

He should get out of this empty house, go for a drive. Perhaps into the hills. He'll take a picnic lunch of honey-ham, hot mustard and ginger beer and try not to worry whether the ham is free-range. He's wrapped the sandwiches neatly in the good-quality baking paper that looks like tracing paper before he remembers that Sue has the car.

Day One, or the first of anything – school, diet, job, no-job, blank page – is always the hardest. He has jumped in without thinking. He needs a plan, a resumé of sorts – his portfolio on a page – that will show the accounts he's held, the campaigns he's worked up, the awards he's won. It's a no-brainer. No more of this *fifteen years with one firm, twenty-five years' experience* nonsense. In this speeded-up world, no one understands – or wants – *multiple years* any more. When he thinks about it, it does sound rather unambitiously static.

Instead. Thought bubble, Ben. He empties the yellow bag in a pile on the coffee table, selects a piece of white chalk, pulls a small rug into the centre of the lounge and sits cross-legged in front of the royal-blue wall they had originally determined would feature a painting they both liked. Well, it won't be a blank blue wall for much longer.

He uncurls himself from the mat, gets up to draw.

By the end of the day, he has a mural – the first draft of a mixed-media 'poster' that turns fifteen years into a colourful tale of tactical triumph. He purchases an electronic list of agencies, drafts a personalised email, photographs the wall in different lights, from different angles. He wishes he could show Sue; he has half a mind to call her. But how much better to call on the back of a job offer.

Checking his inbox, his junk mail box every time he remembers (which is often), starting every time his mobile vibrates in his pocket, he waits a week. While he's waiting he reads a book on salesmanship. Finally he brings the list of names and their phone numbers up on his screen.

'Hi – I was just wondering, enquiring really, whether my poster arrived? You know the one with –'

'Difficult to miss it, buddy. Ben, isn't it? Yes, very clever, we liked it.' He pauses. Ben waits until he can bear the silence no longer.

'Happy to freelance –' He takes a deep breath. 'Or any chance I could drop around for a brief chat? Five minutes. Guaranteed.' His laugh like a skate board on a rough pavement.

'Ben, look. Appreciate your interest, but nothing doing. Keep in touch, won't you.' He's talking to someone else as he hangs up.

It's not going to be easy, Ben says to the lamp. Since when did fly specks look so deliberate? He moves about dusting, sweeping, binning empty wine bottles. Perseverance, that's the important thing. A job is only a job. He wants Sue. But if Sue were here, they'd fight.

There are some wins over the next few weeks. His poster picks up the odd freelance job; when he's busy, time passes and he doesn't notice the passing. The landline rarely rings; when it does, it's for Sue. Very little comes by mail except for bills. He sets the accounts to be paid into one side of the toast rack, those not yet due on the other. There's depressingly little left in the bank and no knowing how long this hiatus will continue.

Outside the sky is cloudless and very blue. It looks warm but spring is unreliable. He shrugs into his duffle coat, sticks his sketch pad in his pocket and on second thoughts takes it out. The park is five minutes in the opposite direction from the bus stop and if ever there was a Sunday to sit and stare, this is it.

From a bench under the spreading arms of an oak he watches the day unfold: hot promises in the eyes of the lovers lying in the longer grass, down by the lake a couple of kids feeding black swans until other children race to join them when there's an altercation about sharing the bread, tears, then distraction as one of the mothers produces a bat and ball. A magpie swoops, pecks and nibbles at something shiny. Sue had been bombed three times in a row by a magpie attracted by her pearl earring, her ear bleeding afterwards not from the peck but from the force of the whack on the side of her head. 'Whomp! Like a cricket ball,' she'd said, her head cradled in his lap with an ice-pack on the sore ear. He smiles, glances across at the lovers, rising now, dusting themselves down and moving off.

He must have dozed because it's predictably cool when he wakes. And empty. Everyone gone, picnickers, kids, birds, even the swans have tucked their heads under their wings. Evidently the maggie had decided its find wasn't of sufficient interest; he nudges it with the toe of his shoe as he passes. A purse delicately fashioned from mesh or chain-mail; he doubts it's silver, but it's pretty.

He picks it up, wonders whether the owner has discovered its loss, slips it deep into the pocket of his jeans, where it feels heavy, the metal cold through the thin calico. He'll return to the park early tomorrow, ask around.

Tonight when he empties his pockets, his fingers close around the silver purse. He's about to fling it on the dresser when he decides to open it. He perches on the edge of the bed, snaps open the clasp, fumbles to bring forth a small pile of silver and a sheaf of green notes that fall about his knees. He wipes the back of his hand across his bristly chin and stares. He counts. Ten of them. He's not too drunk to multiply ten by $100.

A $1,000 windfall. Except it's not his. Except he's taking it back to the park tomorrow. And if she's not there, he's taking it to the police station. That's what you do with lost property: you report it, you drunken drongo. Unsteadily he refolds the notes, collects most of the silver from where it's landed, drops it back in the purse. But there's something else in there, too. A driving licence. With an address. His eyes burn. God damn it Ben, he says. Have you sunk so low you would take what doesn't belong to you?

The owner of the purse lives in the next suburb, about fifteen minutes away. Maybe she won't be home or it could be she no longer lives there? But she does and she is in. A reedy bored-looking woman who, when he asks if she's lost a purse, claims she has, describes it accurately. When he takes the purse out of his pocket and passes it to her, she counts the notes and thanks him. She says, 'Thank you,' smiles thinly.

He stands in front of the firmly closed door for some time. Thank you is not enough. He feels like a courier when he had wanted to feel like Santa Claus. He passes a gleaming car in the driveway, is shocked to feel his hand close around his house key.

In the shredded silence left by a passing motorbike, he's halfway home when he sinks onto a low garden wall – and he stays there until a barking dog moves him on.

There's not much that he remembers between that moment and the next when he finds himself back home calling from the landline.

Babs, the sister, answers. He grits his teeth.

'Well,' she says, 'and if it's not *the voice*.' Predictably. And then not so predictably, 'If you're after your wife, she doesn't live here anymore.' A click. That's it. A day of cheap and effective answers.

He has a rule about not drinking during the day. Even at a wedding breakfast, he will do no more than moisten his lips for the toast. But his rules aren't serving him too well at present. And he needs to think. He's pouring a second glass and thinking around the wisdom of making something to eat when the doorbell rings. He jerks around so he spills the wine. The day before it had been a man with a pink slip, so he ignores it until a few minutes later it rings again. He slams down the glass. Which snaps at the stem.

So when he opens the door to find his wife standing there framed by the wreck of her garden border, which only now he realises he has forgotten to water, his 'Oh, it's you,' comes out as a snarl. Good one, Ben.

She looks well, he thinks, as his vision clears. No, more. Her hair looks different, kinder altogether; her clothes are – sexy.

'You look wonderful,' he says at last.

'Whereas you –' She shakes her head. 'Oh Ben.'

Then she is staring past him over his left shoulder at the poster that covers the wall of their lounge. She looks back up at him and then down at a foil-wrapped object she's holding lightly between two fingers.

'Your ice cream's melting,' she says.

The day so bright it's spilling over.

BABY SHOES

For sale. Baby shoes. Never worn. Six words in the local rag's *for sale* column in bold type with a phone number. That's all. No further information. No price, no clue as to size, colour. Or whether the shoes are for a boy or a girl. It's not till I've thought through the practical bits that the phrase 'never worn' jumps out at me. 'Good as new', 'perfect condition', anything but the black hole of 'never worn'. I swallow. If you were grieving, you just plain wouldn't advertise your baby's clothes. Couldn't. Could you? If the thought came to you, which it wouldn't, you'd puke.

Black tea burns my tongue, tastes like turkey on the inside of my throat. I look across at Rachel. Mischief and angel turn- and frequent turn-about, she is for the moment asleep. From the first I've worked to her rhythm, sleeping or typing while she sleeps, changing and feeding her when she wakes. Yoo-hoo, they'd joked, the crowd I used to hang out with. Single mum! You're brave. She'll turn your life inside-out! Just you wait! Grinning, whooping, rubbing at their tatts. And they weren't wrong. My daughter's birth certainly turned my life back to front, into a place where days and nights swapped and merged and sometimes collided. But it was also a space that was softer and deeper and somehow a lot less lonely than hanging on to the edge of a group where I never really fitted. I've worked out that much.

I bend over the local paper, tracing down the columns with my forefinger, circling a few with the blue pen. Blue is for possibles, red for follow-ups. I bought all my baby clothes and kitted out the nursery by picking up second-hand stuff online, through the paper, at garage sales; you wouldn't believe the stuff people sell for such a low price they might as well put it on the verge, but there is nothing in today's columns of unwanted cots, walkers, baths or strollers I can talk myself into needing.

I'm about to shelve the paper for the compost heap when again the bolded type of **baby shoes** pops out at me. While Rach is too young for shoes at the moment, I suppose it won't be long before she needs them. But what sort of mother would sell her baby's unworn shoes? And what sort of a mother would *buy* them? The mobile is in my hand and the number entered before I think further.

'Hello?' A male voice.

'Hi. You're advertising baby shoes for sale?'

'Wait for her,' he says and thirty seconds later there's a woman's voice the other end. Just then Rachel wakes and over the hullaballoo it's hard to make out a word she says. In the end I ask for the address which turns out to be the next suburb, close enough for a longish walk. Between screams I tell her I'll be there that afternoon. It will provide a focus for our walk and I'm curious. I don't intend to buy, but I tuck ten dollars into my purse anyway. Just in case. But only if they're leather, I promise the Guardian of Rash Purchases who sits on my right shoulder like a ship-surgeon's parrot at times like this. *If* I do happen to purchase them they will be this week's investment in Rach's future.

The unit is closer than I think, but it's uphill and February with the glare as bad as the heat, and when I finally wheel the pram into the porch of the block of flats it's like swimming into one of those delicious cold patches in a soupy sea. When I peek under the muslin cover over the pram, I see Rach's cheeks are bright pink. I bend to kiss her and the skin around her eyes crinkles so she's a miniature of her father staring up at me. She gurgles, throws up her feet and catches at her toes as the sun tosses sparkles into her eyes.

The block is at the meaner end of the suburb, one of those faceless structures where you'd rather not know what goes on behind the bricks. What there is of garden is a spill of bright nasturtiums battling it out with rafts of couch grass, a half-squashed choc milk carton and a trike missing its front wheel. I'm not quite sure why I'm here. I turn the pram so the wheels are facing away down the path, lift the other hand to knock.

The door opens soundlessly and quickly, so that I step sharply backwards to avoid falling forward into the gloom. The man standing opposite is thin and I would have said tall, but it must be the way he holds himself because his eyes are level with mine.

'Sorry to shock you,' he says. 'I am just leaving. But my wife.' He nods to the woman in the hallway beyond him. 'She will put on the kettle. Excuse me.' He inclines his head slightly, touches his embroidered cap and I move aside to let him pass. From the grey in his beard and his deeply scored skin, he would have to be the baby's grandfather. I have no time to wonder who he thinks I might be to deserve a cup of tea because his wife is right there, opening the door wider, ushering me in. Except for the fact that her gown is brown not black, she is dressed like Mother Superior from my convent days. She repeats the invitation.

'No. No, thank you, it's okay,' I say. 'I don't have long. I just came about the baby shoes.' I nod towards the pram. 'I called earlier. Remember?'

'Of course,' she says. 'If you have no time, I understand. Perfectly. In any case, I have them here. Ready.' She turns to a carved hall table, picks up the shoes by the heels and presents them to me on the palm of her other hand. With a sort of flourish as if she's just taken them out from under a locked glass case in a fancy jewellers'.

They look like tiny ballet shoes, white satin or silk with strips of just-pink ribbon long enough to twist around the ankles. That's my first thought: that they're for ballet, until I look again and see the toes encrusted with little pearls, seed pearls both warm and cool, small globes of light that bloom through shades of blue and gold, pink and lilac, that shimmer in a shy way and remind me of the colours of sun on snow or ice.

'But the baby? They were bought for a particular baby? Surely?' I lift my gaze and smile to soften my tone, my eyes. 'Who did they belong to?' I ask. Somehow, I have to know. *Something* I have to know. I am beginning to feel hot on the inside and I wonder again why I'm here.

'No baby,' she says with a smile. 'No baby has worn these.' Her vowels are precise and rather elegantly convincing. She nods again at the shoes, nudges them towards me.

'But, how? How come no baby? How come never worn?' I turn the palms of my hands upwards.

'Festive,' she says, touching the pearly silk with her forefinger. 'For festivity. These are lucky shoes. They will bring your baby good luck, good chance.' She holds them out to me, nods towards the pram. 'Would you like to try?'

'How much?' I need time to decide. I don't know if I can find a use for these. My grandfather used to collect miniature shoes. If he were still alive … But aside from that? I wait for the Guardian to rattle his chain.

'Ten dollars. That's all I am asking.'

'Ten dollars?' I stare at her. I hadn't really thought I'd get them for that. It would hardly pay for the advertisement. They're unexpected. And pretty. But not leather. I promised myself leather. And then another thought arrives on a shaft of sunlight that breaks free from the tree branches and plays on the flimsy wrap over the pram. Rachel moves restlessly. The thought crystallises. I'll have to have her baptised sometime soon. Perhaps, just perhaps, I could make a gown to go with them? With a scattering of pearls on the bodice to match the shoes. Who would come? Who would want to come? Who would *I* want to come? On the other hand, it could just be me and my beautiful kid. And the priest and a special holy candle.

As I continue to hesitate, she turns one of the shoes sideways and I see a small tear in the fabric.

'Only little bit broken, just here.' She touches the small rip lightly. 'That is why I am asking only ten.' She closes her eyes, breathes deeply; it's clear she's disinclined to give further explanation. But quite suddenly I find myself reaching into my bag for the ten dollars, making all the excuses in the world to myself for what is, after all, a luxury purchase and wondering at my quiescent parrot.

I wait while she fusses with a brown paper bag and then there's a movement behind me and he's back again, the man who left earlier.

'I see. You have bought. That is good. A wise purchase.' He moves the muslin aside to look into the pram. There's delight in the stretch of his grin. 'Ah, I see. Here you have a lovely child. The daughter of a strong man.' He stabs at the air with both thumbs.

I wish she was, I think. I wish Rach *was* the daughter of a strong man. Or that the man who is the father of Rachel was stronger than he is. I'm about to trundle my little family back down the hill when something stops me. I look directly at them.

'No man. Just the baby. Just my baby and me.' I shrug.

The man recovers first. 'But never mind. Now you will have luck.'

'I am lucky,' says the woman. 'I have a strong man.' Shyly she glances at him from under the wimple of her cloak.

'And I,' he says. He moves a fraction closer to me, inclines his head, nods at his wife. 'And here you see between us fifty-four years. Fifty-four years we have been together. And the secret? I tell you. The secret is a good woman.' They grin at each other.

When I get home I place the shoes on the mantelpiece. Even if I never use them I can enjoy the skill that went into their making. The small tear, rather than bothering me, reassures me. I guess being less-than-perfect is a good enough reason for rejection from some perspectives, but it's something I've learned to live with. Not a squeak out of my Guardian, so he must agree.

But I can't get the Muslim couple out of my mind and I relive the odd sense of connection that went with my purchase. The woman in her shapeless brown robe with the wimple of her headdress pressing into her forehead. Her husband in his long drab shirt, his colourful cap, the neat silver beard against skin the colour of seasoned teakwood. Fifty-four years. They look young for fifty-four years together. If I added my twenty years to fifty-four, I'd be an amazing seventy-four years old, even if I met my strong man tomorrow.

But am I a good woman? My gaze glances off my mobile sitting on the table in front of me and I still the rising thought almost immediately. Nah. Been too long. Besides, these days I use the phone almost solely for chasing down bargains. But the priest. I could call the priest and see if he's prepared to baptise a child born out of wedlock. And that's what I do and he says how silly of me to think he wouldn't. And is that why he hasn't seen me lately? It is and I tell him so. We set a date for the baptism.

The baptism was going to be just me and Rach until I started on the gown. Ripped up a silk nightdress I'd bought in the days when I thought the clue to fifty-four years of being with someone strong and special was nothing more than a question of seduction. And then gathered a skirt onto a small bodice, added little sleeves and found a shop that sold seed pearls. Just a few and they probably weren't real anyway. When it was finished I arranged the garment against the backrest of my armchair with the shoes peeping out from underneath and snapped a photo on my phone.

And then before I knew it I was dialling home. I spoke first to my mother who started crying so hard she handed the phone to Dad who had trouble, too, and passed me on to my big brother Luke who told me what he thought of me, my child and the child's father and said, 'When can we meet.'

So today with the ceremony over the whole tribe is here, squished into my place and making enough noise for double the number. My child is being handed from person to person like the doll she is and it is not hard for me to see that I've given her back her belonging.

In fact, the only hush in the day is when my sister Fran exclaims so loudly that the crowd slews round to face her. She is holding Rachel in one arm and fingering one of the shoes.

'Been ripped off, babe, you have,' she chortles. She holds up one of Rachel's feet and jiggles her fingernail in the small opening between shoe and sole. 'I don't know where you got these, but they're torn. At least, this one is; there's a slit here in the silk. Look here: it's so neatly done it looks deliberate.'

'They're pretty,' says my cousin, touching one of the pearls. They crowd round, seeing them for the first time, ask me where I bought them.

I tell the small story which suddenly seems very large and they all start speculating at once.

'Bet you they were used to smuggle money,' says Fran.

Luke's all brotherly scorn. 'You nuts? That size? More likely a secret message.'

Unaccustomed to all the attention, Rach squeals and kicks and my mother holds out her arms.

They will bring your baby good luck, good chance, the woman had promised.

On the other side of the room, the Holy Father helps himself to a second glass of champagne and I am so full of the moment that I turn towards the wall – stare at it hard.

NIGHTMARE FARE

It's a strange kid I have in the cab tonight. It's a goodish stretch of road from here to North Beach where she wants to be dropped, so I perve as the highway lights flash her in and out the rear-view. She's striking in a distressed sort of way. Face long and lean, made a darn sight longer by the dangly jobs hanging from her ears. Full lips, but with the too-bright eyes that give me the tip-off that she just might be a user.

I have my window open and the wind shafts a whiff of mint my way. I've learned to pay extra attention to my fares in the later hours and I kid myself I'm an expert at guessing where they're at in terms of fall-out at my expense. Vomit in the back of the car. That and spilt milk. The two worst – apart from the time the chook fell out of someone's shopping bag and cooked at 40-plus in the back of the empty cab on my two days' off. Not something you forget, you'd better believe. But this one looks okay in that department. Just the overpowering smell of mint at odds with the eyes. Unless that's what's on the street these days: mint-flavoured smack.

My left leg starts to cramp and I reach down to rub it hard. Something I hadn't thought about when I first started driving: how tough it would be on the legs, sitting with them stretched out all shift and not moving. They got so bad at one stage I tinkered with giving up the business. Would've, if I'd been able to think of something I liked as much.

'Go to the doctor, why don't you?' She had put it like a question, but after thirty years I knew better. It was the definitive – know what I mean? She has more faith in those medical types than me, my missus.

'"One tablet three times a day and come back and see me in three weeks if you're no better." Is that what you want me to pay good money for? Eh?' I flushed out my coffee mug in the kitchen sink, set it upside -down on the drainer with a bit of a ring.

But when the Lady Babs makes her mind up, there's a choice? So naturally I went. And it turned out I was wrong; this one didn't give me tablets. Told me to take up jogging instead. You could have knocked me over. I'm not one for running, I told him, besides I doubt the ticker would stand up to it. He looked at me, really looked at me, said my heart was just fine, that it was my legs were bad and there were two ways of curing that: Give up driving or take up jogging. Bit tentative at first, but now you can't stop me. Up to 10k on the mornings I'm not driving. For the most part, the legs feel good and I've never felt better.

She's still staring out the window. Nothing much to see on this stretch even if it wasn't night. Could be a uni student. Or a hooker. Or both. Good night for the beach. Hot and sticky. Just right for a dip. Lots of people headed that way early on, though she wants to be dropped further out than most. But it makes for a decent fare this time of night.

'Going swimming?' I ask. I usually talk to my customers. Amazing the connections you make, even on short rides most people are chatty enough. But this one isn't having any of it. Pretends she doesn't hear and continues to stare so intently at the window you'd think it was *Game of Thrones* itself screening there.

We leave the lights behind and are belting along the highway right on the speed limit when I feel a sharp prick in the back of my neck just below the hairline. First up, I think it's a mozzie and I put up my hand to flatten the sucker when I hear a low laugh, almost a chuckle, but pitched high so it sounds crazy – maniacal's the way to describe it – and she starts talking. But the voice that comes out of that painted mouth isn't a woman's voice.

This is the sort of the thing that belongs somewhere else. Somewhere, anywhere, but it was never something I was going to strike for real. Was the jab I felt a needle then? The nutter behind me has started to issue instructions in a weird high-low voice, telling me I'll soon be feeling dizzy and that I'd better pull over, otherwise we're both going to die. Says it over and over in the same creepy voice and I begin to think that if the injection doesn't work, the power of suggestion will. How long do I have before the drug knocks me out? Am I being held up by a man or a woman? This stretch of road has no lights, so now I can't catch sight of the face in the mirror, it's easier to believe it's a man. Have I really been drugged or is this a bluff? The way things are shaping, I have a feeling none of this is going to matter either way.

It's gradually getting through to me that I'm not the one in control here. I don't know whether or not the kid is armed and maybe it's wisest to pull over now, let him take the wheel and see if I can talk him round before the end of the trip? Or to stage a crash and take a chance I'll come out of it okay? But no; I'd take a chance with myself, but not the car. Too much riding on it for that. Not the time to think of the car, nor, right now, about Babs' reaction. Perhaps only a minute has passed since the pinprick, but since then he's rested his knuckles against the back of my neck and I can feel dampness breaking out all over me and my heart trying to climb out of my chest. But I'm fit. I know that. And I can pretend to get dizzy before it comes over me for real. But either my thought processes have slowed or events have speeded up because there's not much pretending needed as the car slews and I slump in my seat.

'Stop fucker. I said stop the car. You fuckin' deaf or summin'?' The pressure on the back of my neck hardens.

I twist to the kerb and it's surprisingly easy to let my head roll back. He has the door open before the car stops and it's not his hand he has pressed against my neck, it's a gun. I swear you can watch versions of cops and robbers all day every day, but nothing quite prepares you for the reality of a gun. The no-two-ways dead-serious end-game menace of it.

From the effort it takes to hoist my body across to the other seat I figure there's not going to be much faking to do. I wonder why he doesn't just push me out and cosh me there and then. Perhaps it's less public where we're heading. The smell of mint is overwhelming as he slides in beside me. He slams the door, guns the car back onto the road leaving a good bit of rubber behind. If he drives like this, we might attract the cops. The radio crackles and from habit I reach for it.

'Get rid of that. Right now,' he says. He rips out the mike, tosses it through the window.

I don't think I've ever been ferried around in my own car. In fact, I can't remember when last I was driven. Barbara always leaves it to me. By now she will be in bed and asleep. My eyes close and I'm thinking back to that ridiculous exchange in the kitchen. And how all she'd said was go see the doctor. Nothing else. With me bracing up for more. And how it wasn't really much to ask.

The car slows, turns sharply to the left. After a short while it turns again and begins to bump and sway so my head wobbles against the head-rest like a baby rattling around in a pram. It's not unpleasant, a bit like when an anaesthetic gets a grip and you give up worrying. I can smell the salt in the air long before the car jerks to a stop. He opens the door just on the curl of a wave so the thumping boom of it comes right in and breaks all over me. The beach, we've reached the beach.

Sound of an engine. A car door opening. Another slamming. People arguing, shouting. Water coming in, going out. Tumbling crash and lisping swish of waves. A thud. Angry voices. Weeping, someone crying, not a woman. My hands might as well be manacled, my eyes blindfolded, for all the help they are. I struggle. That's what I remember, struggle. Struggling. And then running.

Next I know there's a brightness the other side of my closed eyelids. A torch maybe. But brighter than a torch. I wriggle my fingers to find they are cold on my arms and that my arms are gripped like crampons about my chest. I open one eye, wince at the glare, at what might be in front of me.

But the first thing I see is a seagull lift its tail to shit neatly on the bonnet of my car. Both eyes come fully open and I want to wring its bloody neck. Then I realise I haven't run anywhere, that I'm still slumped in the passenger seat, that there might well be someone in the seat behind me – and that the seagull's droppings might be considered somewhat trivial right now. Or, it could be that my luck has changed for the better. It could simply be that.

Ready for a quick getaway perhaps, the car faces away from the ocean back down the way we must have come and I'm gazing into scruffy dunes with the sun coming up over the top. The keys still hang from the ignition. The chaos of the night is still banging around in my head, doubly uncanny set into the calm surrounding me. In fact, it's so quiet that I wonder for an instant whether I imagined it all, whether I'd driven to some pub or other and dropped off the wagon instead of going home to bed. Almost believe I imagined it.

But not quite. Not quite, because there's still a suggestion of mint in the air, stronger than the smell of the sea. Despite the cool of the early morning, it's enough to start the sweat popping. I'm not aware I've been holding my breath until I let it out in small puffs, force myself to turn, to check the back seat, to lean over further to look on the floor.

I twist right around, one way, then the other. Nothing. No movement inside or out. Even the ocean through the rear window is so smooth and untroubled it could be coated with baby oil. Apart from a stiffness in my shoulders, I'm actually unharmed. And thirsty, with the need to piss. Unsure who I'm trying not to disturb, I open the door by degrees, step out onto the sand.

A minute later, I'm back on my side of the car reaching for the door handle, hesitating for less than a second as I think of fingerprints. But that half-second is all it takes for my legs to give way. They give way as

I've always known they would, bending at the knees as if they've been belted from behind by a length of two-by-four so I land on my hands and knees. I sink back, stretch forward, clawing into the sand. I can hear my own breathing and it's not quiet any more.

The car so close, a finger-stretch away. Just a question of willpower. I rest my cheek on the sand. It might be cold and hard on the side of my face right now, but the sun's already warm on the back of my head, so it won't be long before the same stuff heats and melts like liquid glass. I need to get in the car. Even if my legs have given up on me, I can use the horn. Even in this remote spot there must be dog-walkers, joggers, early-morning swimmers. Even here. I heave myself forward. Rest my head again.

As I haul myself up for another try, a shadow slips between me and the sun.

THE TREE'S REAL GIFT

'We want a real tree this year,' my elder son had stated the last time he'd called. 'A proper Christmas tree …' He left his sentence unfinished with the last few words vibrating in my eardrum. My gaze had flickered sideways to the tree I'd just unearthed from the store cupboard. Plastic it may be, but it's also dead-easy to slot in the branches, flick the switch. And then just stand back and watch while the tree goes through its motions like the night view from a hotel window in Singapore. Or the one we had after that and before this, a triangular affair that resembled a church steeple more than it did a tree but which looked pretty decorated with angels and was, I had thought at the time, a good compromise between not getting swallowed up by Christmas and appreciating its ritual.

But this is the year of the Real Tree and the people around me are laughing and joking as if they have just emerged from seeing a funny or uplifting movie.

Only minutes from the city and I'm in the middle of a plantation with trees stretching away from me in every direction. A small group of people cluster around the entrance. Others emerge from an exit balancing their trees on barrows, their children skipping alongside as if it's already Christmas Day. The air itself is loud, zesty. You can taste, smell, the happiness. I find myself smiling. Why didn't I do this in previous years? The kids are due to arrive back from Darwin tomorrow which will give me just enough time to get the tree home and decorated. I have an old copper I can fill with earth, cover with red crepe. I picture their faces, Damien's slight sideways glance because it's uncool to show pleasure or indeed much interest in such things at thirteen, nine-year-old Micky clapping his hands. It will be a good way, I think, to start the holidays.

At the gate, a jovial-looking woman directs people to one of two entrances.

'Do you want to choose today and put a hold on it?' She smiles at me. 'Or cut it down and take it away some other time?'

'Oh, take it straightaway I think. I'd rather not cut it down. I've a plastic bag to protect the roots …' I wave my about-to-be recycled bag.

'Roots? They don't come with roots, darl.' She nods her head towards a line of once-red barrows. 'There's a wheelbarrow and saw for you there, but you might find it easier to choose it first and then come back for the tools.' She hands me a label and a black texta. 'Take these anyway. Just in case.' As I start to move away she calls after me, 'And only those with pink ribbons are available.'

But a felled tree? For some reason I hadn't anticipated that. I glanced again at the check-out queue seeing now what I'd somehow missed earlier – that all the trees had been severed from their roots. I'd part-filled the copper with dirt already and there was a space in one corner of our garden where I had thought I might plant it out when it had done its job. We could have a tree-planting ceremony, be proud that we hadn't contributed to waste and celebrate that we now had a sort of everlasting tree that we could decorate *in situ* the following year, and the year after that. I had pictured it glowing brightly all around the suburb. But maybe Christmas trees don't come like that anymore – built-in obsolescence in this business too.

I know it's way too late to start looking for alternatives, but I wonder whether this will fill the brief of a 'proper' tree. Next year I'll go to a plant nursery instead of the advertised Christmas tree plantation. Besides, they don't have to know it has no roots, do they? It'll still look real. Determined to sidestep an impending guilt trip, I turn for reassurance to the smiles on the faces of young and old alike as I join the hunt for the perfect tree.

A sign at the beginning of each row sets out instructions for choosing the trees. As I have been told, only those with pink ribbon ties are available; trees already sold carry the buyer's name and I find that some of the best-looking specimens carry no tag at all. It's the third day of Christmas already and the ground is packed with avid hunters. I move quickly from row to row.

My eyes get used to spotting pink tags. I wander from possibility to possibility. Am I being too fussy? The trees are too small to provide much shelter. I begin to wish I'd brought a hat. Above me is the uncompromising savage blue of the Perth sky that I miss so much when I'm away, but even so, somehow it doesn't feel like Australia. In fact, it occurs to me that it doesn't feel like anywhere I've ever been. It's an overwhelming sky that hangs like an inverted fishbowl over this woodland of small trees, most of which stand only a little taller than me. The way the sound is filtered out lends a disorienting sensation as if I'm trudging in a paperweight, as if I'm not quite in control of this rather exciting method of choosing the perfect tree and that any moment I might be turned upside down to disappear in a flurry of pine needles. A pity the children aren't here to experience this with me. This never-never land of Christmas trees. I berate myself for wanting the surprise to be in place, for not thinking it through properly. And then wonder why I hadn't come out in the cool of early morning instead of the heat of midday. I trip over something, glare at a jagged stump.

When I finally get my almost-perfect tree home, I find there's a branch missing towards the bottom. I untie the ropes, lug it off the roof rack. It had turned out to be easy enough to saw through the trunk, but the tree was heavier than I had expected and the hard part now is getting it upstairs without further damage. In the end I roll it onto an old blanket and tug the parcel up the stairs.

Finally I prop it against the wall and flop into the nearest chair. The tree looks as exhausted as me, not exactly smaller than before but less of a tree than it had appeared in location. It's flattened on one side from its journey and it's also dropping needles. Already. Water, I hope, will set it right. 'Earth?' The cheery-looking woman had glanced at me, her fingers tap-tapping away at the cash register. 'No, no earth in the pot, luv; water is what these need. Like one of those watering pots you see behind you.' I had withstood the temptation to double the price of the purchase: the old copper I had at home was sound, the copper would do just as well.

So now, once I've caught my breath, with some difficulty I dump the dirt, fill the tub with water, then – somehow – holding the tree with one hand, wedge it with rocks. I let go gingerly, stand back. Hope the wound it's suffered finds solace in the wet.

It's easy enough to place the flat part to the wall, to cover the battered old tub with crepe, but after that I have more trouble. The branches look even enough but the harshness of the tinsel clashes with this real tree, lending it an incongruity that is suggestive, somehow, of a once-lively face in a pink satin-lined coffin.

It is clear to me that tinsel is not going to work. Nor do the glitter-coated angels, altogether too small and insignificant for so large a tree. I settle for baubles which have to be coaxed onto the drooping ends of the branches and held fast with wire. I find a drape of lights at the back of the store cupboard, wind them here and there. Unwind. And start again. Halfway-through, I turn on the light in the lounge. When it's finished I have to admit that it's far from the artistic creation I'm aiming for. It looks – awkward. And very, very clumsy. Perhaps I've lost the knack of decorating a real tree. Perhaps I never had it anyway. I have another go with the tinsel. Top it with a foil star. At least the glass baubles make me smile. They remind me of ones we had when I was a child – some are red, kind of like upside-down hot-air balloons, others clear with old-fashioned embroidery stuck on, some are gold, others like silver ice cream cones.

I switch on the lights of the almost-real tree, turn off the house lights, sit in the dark sipping my glass of wine. By the time I go to bed, my creation blazes in front of me as if lit by a thousand splendid candles.

My children arrive home the next morning. We have a late breakfast on the porch. Conversation starts and stops. The children examine the Tree.

'It doesn't look like a real Christmas tree. It's the wrong sort,' says Damien exchanging glances with his brother.

'Well, it's a pine tree,' I say in my most reasonable voice. 'Christmas trees are pine trees. After all.'

They digest this. They say, 'But it's sort of – uneven. And there's a bare bit at the back.' They say something like that. Or do I imagine it?

I look at the Tree. The particular green of the needles and the baubles merge. In daylight, the pinpricks of the lights are somewhat overshadowed by the ugly black wire that strings them together.

'Well, naturally it's not perfect because it's not an artificial tree, you see. It's a real tree. Reality isn't perfect.' My voice sounds as crunchy as cornflakes. I glare at my elder son. Who gazes at his sibling as he says, 'Since the star is not a real planet, the tinsel is not real snow and the baubles not real presents, why have a real tree?' He eyeballs me and I wonder where I went wrong.

They discuss their recent trip with their father to Disneyland, mention Doreen twice.

'Doreen? Who's Doreen?' I ask into one of the gaps.

'Oh, just someone Dad knows,' says second son, Micky, slicing his toast into chessboard squares.

'She's not just *someone he knows*. She's his *friend*. Dummy.'

They glower at each other. I go to ask, 'Is she nice?' Until I realise it's not what I want to know at all.

After breakfast I call the tree woman. Tell her that the tree is less than a day old and it looks terrible.

'Did you purchase one of our containers?' Her voice has lost its smile. She sounds tired.

'Well, no. No, I didn't. But I put it straight into water as soon as I got it home. It droops. And it's shedding needles. Badly. Already.' The tone of my voice higher than usual.

'The best thing to do is to take it outside and give it a thorough drenching. That'll freshen it up.'

'But it's upstairs. And decorated. I really don't think I could face …'

There's a pause.

'You could try misting it. Or hairspray sometimes helps …'

I thank her and hang up.

Christmas comes and somehow goes. We try outings – the zoo, roller-blading, the science museum. I have something planned for each day until it becomes clear that the boys are traipsing around to please me when in reality Damien has two favourite modes of being – listening to music in his room or lounging in front of the television – while Micky is completely absorbed with his iPad.

The tree lurks in the corner. Despite the fact that I top up the water every two days, it looks rather more grey than green and the needles are gathering on the floor in an unsettling manner. I contemplate calling the plantation again to ask what I might do to encourage it to last until Twelfth Night – sugar perhaps or aspirin – but something tells me there is no happy answer.

January 6th has never taken so long to arrive. I'm loading the tree onto a trolley when my elder son appears from his room. It's nearly lunchtime and he's dressed as if for bed, but we have this wobbly set of Rules and Conditions between my ex-husband and me that leaves both of us uncertain and the children confused. So beyond my hello smile I don't say anything. He watches while I lug the tree downstairs and out the door. But he doesn't see my face as I tumble it up against the fence.

I'm so sorry, I say to the tree. Sorry you had to sacrifice yourself unnecessarily. Sorry I was so ready to cut you from your roots. What a waste, not only that you had to die so I could feel good about myself in front of my boys, but that you had to be a part of our whole abortive attempt at merry-making.

There is no movement from the tree, but it's no longer dropping needles, and in some strange way it seems to be listening. I stand there a long time.

It's only when I turn back towards the house I find myself wondering whether Damien had understood what I had said in defence of the tree the day they had arrived.

Reality's rarely perfect, I had snapped. Something like that. But I wonder whether I really understand that myself? After all, hadn't I tried to plan the perfect time together? Hadn't I made an effort to get a real tree? Was I expecting a miracle then? A seamlessly happy holiday with two boys who were quite probably feeling just as uprooted themselves? What sort of wonderland was I living in? How could I expect my children to understand a concept I had obviously not grasped myself?

By the time I'm back up the stairs, Damien's in his second-favourite position staring hard at the television, his headphones over his ears, his feet on the coffee table. I walk across the room, flick off the set.

'What did you do that for?' He doesn't move his gaze from the blank screen.

I sit in the armchair opposite.

'Listen, Damien,' I say. 'Listen to me.'

I tell him about the fairyland of trees, about my excitement when I first arrived at the plantation followed by my disappointment when I discovered it was to be a cut tree. I talk about the waste, the waste going on right now in lots of homes across the world as they throw out their dead trees. About my hope that we could have planted it out and decorated it together next year and how, the year after that, we'd have needed a ladder.

'I hate plastic, too,' I said. 'But what's a better way of doing trees? And of doing Christmas altogether? How can we improve on things – on everything – for next year? So we all have a better time. What do you think?'

Slowly he lifts his feet off the table. He takes off the headphones and turns his head to look at me. Really looks. He starts to talk.

MIDDLE MAN

Being winter – and a cold and miserable one at that – Bill was not unhappy when the bloke who lived in the end villa knocked on his door to ask if he'd like his morning paper once he'd finished with it.

'I get it delivered each day anyway,' he said, holding it out. 'So, if you like, from now on I can hang a shopping bag just outside my door and leave the paper there when I'm through. That way you can collect it whenever it's convenient.'

Most of the residents kept to themselves, but Dave was a busy-looking man with a short well-trimmed moustache who'd taken it upon himself to keep the complex neat and tidy, so Bill had often seen him round and about.

'Absolutely delighted. Can't think of a better way to start the day, particularly these cold mornings. Do you want it back afterwards?' And when Dave shook his head, he continued, 'Tell you what then. I'm happy to pay for it. That way you get something back.'

They shook hands, a firm business-like grip that sealed the deal. From that morning on, each time Bill collected the paper he left one gold and one silver coin in its place at the bottom of the green bag.

Since Joyce had died, breakfast had been the low spot of the day, but now all because of this small adjustment, he found he could turn it into a small ceremony instead. Each day, once he'd collected the paper, he would place it on the breakfast bar beside his four pieces of toast, butter, marmalade and jug of coffee, slip his one-egg omelette onto a warm plate and settle down to eat and read. The complex faced east and so while the units were chilly during the long days, this time of the morning there was a sliver of sun that settled at the centre of his back and widened as the days got longer.

Sometimes there was a small square missing from the paper where Dave had clipped out an advertisement, sometimes a rectangular gap in the deaths or memoriam columns and Bill came to expect this, feeling after a while that in some small way, through what was missing, he was getting to know him, starting to make a friend. And then when he himself, well over an hour later, had finished reading, he recycled this largesse by passing it on to the man in the unit next door, a tall terse fellow with a glass eye and Polish-sounding name he knew only as Rolf. Takes a while to make friends, he told himself. Small steps.

The argument erupted with such unexpected ferocity that at first Bill thought it was the dogs up the road who'd slipped their leads to have a bit of a dust-up. He went to the window, angling the slats of the blind so he could peer through, and up there by the bins were Dave and Rolf having a real spat. One slammed his clenched fist on the bin, the other kicked it sharply before spinning away and striding off down the road.

The next time Bill came across him, Dave was still angry. 'Can't stand that man. Interfering old bugger. I'd be obliged if you'd quit giving my newspaper to him.'

'Well … well, Dave, I don't know about that. It's not my quarrel and I don't want to buy into the middle of it. Besides, since I pay you for the paper, strictly speaking it's mine to do what I like with …'

'All the same.' Dave pushed out his chest.

But Bill could be stubborn, too. Furthermore, like everything else that had happened in his life so far, he was convinced the disagreement would pass and that everything would continue as usual. And, it did, for the remainder of that week. Then when he fronted up at Dave's door the following Monday, the bag was empty. He stood scratching his head for a long moment. Then thinking something untoward might have happened to the man who was shaping up to be his friend, he knocked.

The door swung open and there was Dave with his arms crossed just as if he had been standing behind it, waiting.

'I've stopped the newspaper,' he announced.

'Uh? Stopped it? I see. Oh dear. From when?'

'From yesterday.'

'Ah. Ah, I see. Just like that.'

'Just like that. G'day.' Dave nodded briefly and the door closed as smoothly as it had opened.

Bill stood outside gazing at the shut door and at the empty bag which trembled on the handle for a minute or so before it stopped dancing, before it became clear that the door wasn't going to open again, that Dave wasn't going to bring out the newspaper from behind his back to say with a grin, 'Just joking. Had you that time, didn't I?'

Pulling back his shoulders, he turned away. Well, in that case, I can get it delivered myself, he said aloud. But he knew it wasn't that. It wasn't just the paper.

Back inside his unit, the triangle of sun was missing entirely that morning and the room looked quite different, almost as if he had occupied it for the last six months without living in it.

I'll go for a walk, he thought. Get out of the place. Treat myself to a cup of coffee down by the water. He closed the door on his curling omelette and in twenty minutes he was down by the sea.

He picked one of the less ostentatious coffee shops and, finding himself the only customer, took a seat by a window wondering as he did so whether the vinyl table and the dull pewter-grey of the view in front of him was really any cheerier than his villa. Someone appeared, looking as grumpy as he felt himself.

'We're not open,' said the man abruptly. 'Don't open until eight Mondays.'

'Uh. Well, in that case I'll come back in half an hour. I'm only after a hot drink, cup of coffee …'

The man shuffled his feet.

'Is that all? Flat white? In that case, no problem …'

'No, no, don't worry.' Bill was on his feet. 'I'll go for a bit of a walk. Back soon.'

A beach suburb has only two seasons, he reflected, the swinging summer with its crowds and rowdy music and the soulless stretch of the cooler months when it resembles a type of purposeless wasteland.

The café had been warmer than he thought, and a breeze had started up, so once down on the beach he wrapped his arms around his body. The only people out today were the hardy types swimming close to shore and the inevitable dog-walkers, always undeterred by weather. Perhaps he should get another dog? Unlikely they'd allow that in the complex. Not with Dave fussing about. The empty bag quivered at the periphery of his vision. Perhaps he should have made more of an attempt to find out what was wrong. Played peacemaker. Angry, suddenly, that his thoughts returned so easily to Dave and Rolf, he swung his arms free, quickened his pace.

When he returned, the café was still empty. The table he'd sat at earlier was set now with a cup of steaming coffee, a croissant with a pat of butter and small dish of orange marmalade he could taste on his tongue just by looking at it. Resting on the side plate, neatly folded, was the Monday newspaper. He hesitated. The waiter appeared from the kitchen and Bill thought he came close to smiling when he saw him standing there in a bit of a dither not knowing whether to sit or move on.

'Let me know if you want anything else.' He nodded briefly at the table, ducked back the way he'd come.

For the next hour, the only interruption was a couple who arrived squabbling and left arm in arm. The paper long since read, he continued to sit, gazing towards a horizon missing altogether that day. The sound and smell of hot oil wafted through the open door to the kitchen; from time to time the coffee machine gurgled. A woman emerged from a back room and started sweeping up the papers eddying in the far corners of the room. When she felt his gaze on her, she propped the broom against the wall.

'You 'bout ready to go, then? That'll be $3.50. Boss-man says the croissant's on the house to make up for his snappiness earlier. Staff let him down again, so what does he do? Calls in his unpaid labour of a mother, doesn't he?' She took a quick look around the café. 'Nothing much happening here. Mind if I take the weight off my feet?' She dropped into the chair opposite. 'And you? What's got a chap like you out and about at this still unholy hour of a wintry morning?'

He moved in his chair, looked down at the table, shifted his gaze back to the ocean. Only six months of silence and his tongue had forgotten its moves. She shrugged, smiled briefly, and he had the feeling she wasn't one to stick around where she wasn't wanted. He winced as the clouds parted and the surface of the sea responded with a glare as bright as a hot tin roof. What was he doing here anyway?

'It's me mates, you see,' he finds himself saying. 'Neighbours, to be exact, not quite mates. But over the months, it's become like they're friends. They've had a quarrel and it makes things a bit tight in the small space. We didn't have kids, see, Joyce and me. And now she's gone …'

He began to tell her. But once he started talking he found he didn't want to stop – and that Dave and Rolf were only a small part of what was on his mind.

DONOVAN

Left to itself, the forest was a still place, thought Donovan. Not silent or untenanted, but uncomplicatedly tranquil in the way that a river appears still on a windless day. It was his presence in their territory that brought the flies out into the late afternoon heat, that set up the occasional rustle in the scrubby growth to the side of the track, that turned the vibration of his tread into an echo that flirted with the grass trees and played in the tops of the tall gums that lorded it over the lot. He skirted a snake coiled to one side of the path, wondering at first whether it was dead, why it didn't move, why its mouth was jammed open as if with a stick until he realised it was in the process of digesting a frog. Strips of sunlight flickered on his head and shoulders; fickle patterns of light and shade converged and camouflaged like combat dress with the trees themselves in on the act.

It seemed to the ranger watching from the high ground outside his hut that the young man climbed the track as if he had a load of granite in his pack.

As he drew closer, the ranger saw he was older than the youths the Department usually sent; he was just twenty perhaps, no longer a boy, but somehow not quite a man. And perhaps his initial thought about the heavy pack had been off-target; at a guess the heaviness came from somewhere else entirely. He guessed, too, from the way the bloke's ripped T stretched at his chest, that he had the potential to be a good worker. And that was all he needed, or indeed wanted, to know.

The young man walked right up to where he stood in front of the wood hut, so close his shadow had moved beyond the ranger before he stopped to shrug the pack from his shoulders. He raked his fingers through the sweat of his spiked city haircut, stuck out his hand.

'The name's Donovan,' he said, his voice tight, the light blue of his eyes cloudy, opaque and not quite seeing as if they'd be more comfortable behind thick glasses. 'You're expecting me.'

The ranger nodded, just one movement of his head. Slowly he drew a creased leather pouch from the back pocket of his jeans and a roll of papers from his shirt pocket.

'Smoke?' he asked, and his raised eyebrow gave his wrinkled face a lopsided look.

'You wouldn't catch me smoking even if …' Donovan started. He tossed his head, shrugged off his pack.

The ranger looked at him for a long moment before squatting to roll his cigarette. Problem is, this is a desert island, mate.

Aloud he said, 'Too late to do anything tonight. Wind's getting up. Want to toss your gear in that cabin there, take a look round? Down the valley, other side of that hill there, is a bit of a lake. If you're lucky you might snag a trout. Fishing tackle's in the shed. We'll fry up something to eat a bit later and start in on some planting. Gotta spray too. Lantana's gotten a hold since some nutter started a fire.' He shuttered his eyes against the last of the sun, squinted up at the young man. 'That suit?'

Donovan kicked out at a stone. His toe caught at the edge so it spun and shot off at an angle to bounce off the side of the cabin. He turned to face the ranger.

‘I don’t do fishing.’ His lips curved into his chin. ‘Anything else, but not that.’ He scooped up his pack with one hand and flung it into the hut. Aided by the wind, the door slammed behind him with a sharp crack.

The ranger lightly rolled his smoke. He slid his tongue along the gummed edge, pressed paper to paper, placed the cylinder in the corner of his mouth and bent his head to the flare of the match. His hands unsteady. For an uneasy moment back there, he had thought the kid was going to cry. They certainly sent him variety. The ones on drugs, the committed greenies, the lazy bastards happiest when they were lounging on a bush turkey mound and once there was a girl – pretty lass she was too – who’d worked her butt off. Top gun was the young man who came from the far north, from the Kuku Yalanji people, though he’d never quite worked out what had tempted him so far south.

He drew hard on his cigarette, held the smoke a fraction of a second longer than usual. Donovan was your typical over-heated young bloke who thought he was different and wasn’t. He’d remain angry, too, Donovan would, until someone showed him that he was just another thorn on the stem. The world was full of Donovans. But Donovan wasn’t his business. Donovan was here to do a job. And, if he’d let himself, to learn something along the way.

Turned out Donovan was a worker. The ranger had been right about that. Once the lad had cleared a break of the big stuff, he set to with a scythe and hacked along the edges, worked till the blisters popped up on the thumb and palm of his right hand. He switched to the left and said nothing and the ranger said nothing, but the next day both hands were bandaged with strips of cloth and he cut and slashed at twice the speed. He worked till his hair lifted without the gel and until there was more rip than cloth on his back. They said little, but there was a rhythm to what they did as if it had always been that way, the cutting and clearing, the tagging and notching of trees in trouble.

In the mornings the ranger rose when the sky showed colour and had the kettle boiling and the eggs frying before Donovan woke. Time was, the ranger thought to say, when this here was a billy and not a kettle, but the effort of telling didn’t seem worthwhile. They ate like they worked, without fuss, mopping up the grease with bread, washing it down with milky tea thick with sugar, rising together to rinse the mugs and plates. And then they would be off, the ranger carrying the packed lunch of bread and butter, a tin of corned beef, a flask of tea and a half-packet of gingernut biscuits, while the younger man shouldered the tools. Ten days passed that for the ranger were like most other days of the past years, a comforting passage of work and sleep. He paid no more attention to Donovan than he had to any of the students, but occasionally he felt the younger man's gaze rest on him and for reasons he preferred to keep to himself, he was disturbed.

'Feet of clay,' he caught himself muttering. 'Feet of clay here, sonny. Poke me, I'll fall over.'

He noticed that Donovan's antipathy to fishing didn't extend to the catch itself which he cooked and ate with lusty relish. He was pretty good at cleaning the trout, too – expertly rubbing off the scales, slitting, gutting, rinsing.

One late afternoon, almost at the end of the stay, the ranger was grilling a trout, turning it gently round and round as if on a spit, letting the fire flame to its body oils and crisp its skin while his mind stayed back on the fight with it, so when Donovan spoke he started.

The lad was sitting in his usual way – cross-legged on the hard-packed clay – stabbing at the ground with his penknife. As the ranger looked across at him, he blew out his breath as if it had no right to be where it was. 'Hell,' the youth repeated, meeting his gaze. 'I have to talk to somebody … if I don't …' He dropped the knife, reached for a twig, snapped it once, twice, again and again until it had multiplied into a pile of kindling.

The ranger sighed. Sometimes they got talkative. He much preferred the silent evenings, but he'd come to respect the way this bloke worked. Besides there was something in his tone that he found difficult to ignore. He turned the fish and the fire sizzled and spat until he dropped it in the pan to finish off. Bloody greenies, all the same.

'You bored with being up here or something?'

'No mate. Nothing to do with being here. Up here, it's not real.'

'Ah.' The ranger peered over the smoke and for the first time saw the light-coloured eyes looking straight into his. 'Ah,' he said again. He looked away, first up into the trees and then back down at the trout, saw he was in danger of overcooking it. Suddenly he was afraid for Donovan. Afraid, because he had no answers for himself, let alone anyone else.

He flipped the first fish onto a metal platter, dropped the second into the pan and made a show of being busy with a fire that didn't need tending. After a few minutes, he heard Donovan draw a deep breath.

'Sickness, pain, death. Is that what's at the end of all this? Is that all there is? After all the striving? It's like intricate mandalas made of coloured sand being dumped in that lake of yours down there. It doesn't make any sense to me.'

'You paint a pretty bleak picture. Sure it's bad as all that?' The ranger strove to keep his tone light, to deflect what he knew was coming. They all wanted to change the world. Nothing wrong with that. Once he had been as fierce. But the issues were the same. And nothing much did change. Same old problems kept coming up like a bad run at cards. Solved. Dissolved. Returned. And then solved and dissolved all over again.

'As bad as all that? What could be worse than …' Donovan stopped mid-sentence as if the air had been let out of his body. He pushed himself to his feet where he stood waving a little as if he were drunk or drugged.

The ranger wanted a cigarette, but this was not the time with Donovan standing there with his face all twisted up.

For a moment he wondered whether he had been putting too much onto him, making him work too hard. Whatever it was, the bloke looked as though he was having some sort of a breakdown. He wasn't thinking quite straight himself for that matter. Usually he opened a can of beans to accompany the meal. He looked down at the trout. What he didn't intend was for these little beauties to go to waste – it wasn't as though they'd jumped onto the hook. Much longer and they'd start to congeal on the plate and the slight wind that had just started up wasn't helping any.

But then, so what? There was more at stake than a couple of fish and the longer he kept up the façade of their usual routine, the better. Relying partly on this attempt at normality and Donovan's healthy appetite to restore the balance of the day he took his time to rake through his little store for the beans, divided the can between the two plates and added a few biscuits for good measure. A mug of milky tea – that had been his wife's panacea for death, disaster and everything else – and that would have to do for now. He'd make a new batch of damper later that evening.

He was conscious of acting like a bird, his entire attention apparently concentrated on what he was doing – slicing off the fish heads, removing the vertebrae with another flick of the knife, sliding one of the trout onto another plate – while all the time he kept the lad clearly in his sights. Usually this was Donovan's job: the ranger caught the fish; Donovan cleaned, cooked and served.

'Here we are,' he said at last. He nodded at the plates. 'Let's tuck in.' While Donovan slumped into a chair, the ranger kept talking. 'We're out of fish. I'll have to make time for the lake tomorrow.' He raised his eyebrows. 'Feel like coming? Last chance before you leave.'

'Like I told you. I don't fish.'

'That's hard to believe when you like the stuff so much.' Slowly the ranger chewed on another tasty mouthful while, inside his chest, he felt his heart rattle.

The boy's eyes blazed briefly. He opened his mouth and the ranger braced himself.

But what he was saying was smothered in the rush and clatter of a flurry of cockatoos that swirled into the clearing. The ranger longed to rise to their challenge, to throw up his arms as he did when he was alone, to throw back his head and shake his fists, to yell, 'Yaa, yaa, yaa! Yaa, yaa, yaa!'

But right now, his sight was fixed on the movement of the boy's distorted lips, the sounds forced, he could see, through a fug of pain and possibly shame. As he watched, he thought he caught a word here and there, but gradually the words became less important. Because, after all, in some situations, what were words but a poor attempt to describe the indescribable. And then the boy widened his eyes, raised his voice, so it reached higher than the birds even, he must be yelling now, the single word lake, lake, lake filtered through the din – until the ranger understood enough to recognise the depth of his grief and to know that on a lake some place, something very bad had happened to someone Donovan loved. When the talking stopped, something inside the ranger shifted gear to some half-remembered sense that had started to function, a sense that could better understand how it felt to be alive when you wished with all your heart that you were dead. A sense that could understand that it wasn't wicked to feel like that – but very, very human. Above and around them, the forest reverberated until when at last the parrots realised the ranger was not going to play, their gaming changed to protest and they dipped and wheeled away to become a distant squawking, their wide white wings a signature strung across the westering sky.

The ranger went to say something in the sudden silence and stopped. What, after all, was there to say?

After some time, it was Donovan who spoke first. 'You're at peace with yourself, aren't you?' He picked up a piece of bark as if to do something with his hands, his eyes.

The old man pushed his plate aside, reached for his smokes. He shrugged. 'I wouldn't put it quite like that. We've all got stuff's happened to us. Good and bad happens. For all of us, in each generation at one time or another, it's a question of putting one step in front of the other, taking things a day at a time. Each generation trying to figure out a good reason for being here, each searching for something, picking over the tailings for what might have escaped the one before.

'Except, that is, for my generation and my old man's, we had the wars, you see, and there's nothing quite like a war to stop you searching and turn you around to facing. Because once you've done your manly duty and shot into the jungle, shot down a man before he got you or the chap alongside – or stumbled across your best mate with his head a long way from his body – there's something set up in you for keeps, you see, and your dreams … your dreams.' He blew out his breath.

'Best way I can describe it is if my life was a book writ down and set before you, there'd be big chunks of it you'd find gummed up …

'At peace with myself? Is that really how it seems to you?' His breath caught and he turned away to cough hard into his handkerchief.

It was rare that a smoke had the effect of stealing his breath, but he ground out what was left of the cigarette nonetheless. He was strangely tired. Perhaps he too had overdone it in trying to keep up with the young chap. He raised his eyes to the tangled canopy of growth above him and it helped somehow that what he could glimpse of the sky had a tinge of summer blue with the last of the day's sun glinting hotly through the leaves.

'Take it easy, son,' he said. 'You're wound too tight. Often we spend our time trying to fix life only to find it's not broke after all.' But as he rose to clear away the remainder of the meal, his hands shook.

The next day, Donovan was ready to leave. He hefted his pack and stepped into the open. The old man felt for his pouch.

Just as he'd done when he arrived, Donovan dipped his head and ran his fingers through hair that had by now grown out of its spikes. He shook the ranger's hand.

'Be seeing ya,' he said.

The ranger gave up trying to pull forth the tobacco. All the talk of searching and thinking had stolen his sleep the night before and already the day had a jagged edge to it. He had a fierce urge to step towards Donovan, to clasp his shoulder, hug him even, but he pulled himself back. Instead he heard himself saying, 'Well, it won't be the same with you gone. Come back some day. Come back and see us some day, eh?'

Was it the right or the wrong thing to say? He had a feeling he would never know. The youth nodded, turned and set off down the path.

The ranger made another attempt to reach for his cigarette papers, but the coughing started just as the kookaburras began their warble. First one, then another and another of the blinkin' birds dissolving into raucous laughter until it seemed like the whole forest was collapsing about him. He dropped the tobacco where he stood, clapped his hands to his ears and stumbled into the hut.

Donovan had almost reached the point where the track ended at the main highway when he heard a sharp crack, loud enough to set off the birds again. The door, perhaps? The metal door caught by the wind?

Hesitating at the junction, he frowned and turned to look back up the path. Strange old fucker. He'd looked a bit shaky back there. He was about to go on, when the old man's words came back to him. *At peace with myself? Is that how it seems to you?*

Surprising himself with the depth of his sigh, he shrugged his pack higher only to stand gazing for some time at the highway that snaked down to the city. The forest had returned to silence by the time he turned to start back up the hill.

'OWZAT!'

It's late in the season. Hot. The ground is crisp as old bread beneath its thin crusting of grass with the afternoon sea breeze holding off. A stinker of a day altogether, you could say, with the end-of-season temperature reaching for a new record. When and where they can, the fielders skulk in the shade of the peppermint trees. From time to time the captain calls them in and they overreact, running too briskly to cover their reluctance.

There is only one umpire this match when there should be two. But it can't be helped. One is better than none, they said. Anyway, we don't have a choice. We'll go ahead with one. Just as good really.

But the umpire himself is not so sure that it's just as good. Not too sure at all. There's a synergy of decision created by one-plus-one that adds up to a sense of comfort. He feels too prone to fallibility standing alone in his hot black-and-white costume at the head of the pitch. It's nearly two hours into the innings with two to go. Under the thick dark serge of his trousers, a line of sweat tickles as it travels down the inside of his thigh.

Holding the bowler's cap behind his back, he stands with body taut and head thrust forward, lining up wicket with wicket, narrowing his eyes like a dog with the neighbour's cat in its sights. Flies drop under the brim of his hat to suck at the wet of his forehead and he slaps at them absently, bending still lower as first he senses, then feels, the vibrations that tell him the bowler has started his run. He hears a short grunt as a flash of red, blurred to brown with the speed of it, hurtles past his left ear, hits the pitch and rolls harmlessly to off side. The batsman straightens, stretches his spine, drops back down over his bat.

The umpire clicks the counter in his left hand, tugs at his collar, feels almost dizzy as his concentration breaks. His jaw aches and he wonders why it should be his jaw and not his head. He lengthens his gaze to where a group of children are playing tag in and out the avenue of peppermint trees, but he doesn't really see them, just hears their yells. Why do children shriek so? One run of the 29th to go. Time for another three or four overs before tea. Thirteen minutes to tea break.

They don't always happen, but when they do, you can't beat the ladies' teas. He teases his taste-buds with a vision of plates stacked with neatly controlled triangles of white bread filled with thin-sliced ham and mustard, or glued together with anchovy paste or mushy egg. Sees piles of scones still steaming beside jugs of cold cream and home-made strawberry jam. Smells the sweetness of the milky tea. But he knows it's just as likely to be warm water from his bag along with half a buttered muffin saved from lunch.

The batsman crouches and the ground starts to rumble. The umpire tenses. He leans forward as the ball whizzes by, watches keenly as the batsman swings across his body at the rising ball. The leather bounces sweetly off the willow to loft towards the boundary. For four.

A small cheer. 'Good on ya, mate!' from the supporters lolling in the rectangle of shade beside the pavilion. The bowler swipes at the sweat with his sleeve, puts out his hand for his cap. The umpire waits until the young man meets his gaze, eye to eye.

'Thanks, umpie,' he says. And gets his hat back.

When the umpire changes ends, he is facing into the peppermints and the sun gets a chance at the other side of his face. Hat, sunscreen, sunglasses – all the slip slap slop – and his face still raw the next day. He remembers he had a beard to keep the sun off his cheeks when he was a kid working the wheat bins. That was a long time ago. His attention returns as the next bowler holds out his cap.

'Be much obliged, ump, if you'd hang onto this for me.' Sometimes they ask, often they don't. Makes a hell of a difference if they do. You don't feel so isolated. His mind is wandering again and he forces it back. Takes the cap with a curt nod. Everyone in position. Raises and lowers his right arm.

The ball is a good one, served well up to the batsman. The umpire squints, bends towards the wicket. It takes a fraction of a second for the ball to snap away at an angle. Too fast for the human eye to follow. His ears strain for an echo. No wood involved. Too low for the glove. Must have come off the pad.

Out LBW. He signals, but the batsman had started walking before his arm went up. A small thrill trembles through him. Good sportsmanship always affects him this way. But relief he made the right decision comes at the same time and the sweat breaks through his hat band stinging his left eye before he knuckles it out. A fly sticks to the corner of his mouth. Always tricky, these LBW decisions.

The next bat is a tall thin player who looks like a stick insect once he hunkers low. Again the ball. The batsman steps neatly aside, swings his bat out of the way, allows the ball to sail harmlessly by. The next delivery. Again the ball deflects and again no woody click. But this time there's a gleeful shout from the bowler: 'Owzat!'

The umpire senses the collective tension of the fielders swing towards him as they wait for his sign, while those closest begin their move to congratulate their team-mate. Slowly the batsman stands upright.

The umpire debates. The pressure is on him to make a decision in less than the time it takes to swallow. His mouth is dry, his shirt wet. The ball had appeared to bounce off higher than the pad. Off the glove perhaps? Or the body? He calls on his lifetime of play to aid his combined sense of sight and sound. The last part of the scene replays in his mind. Five seconds pass. Five seconds is a long time for a decision. Too long. They are waiting. Watching him like a class of kids waiting to know who won first prize. Again he replays the ball, fighting his memory for exactness. At the height it was when it bounced away, it was more likely to have come off the glove than the body. The glove is seen as part of the bat. He decides. Signals. Not out.

'What the deuce?' The bowler's face reddens, his arms suddenly slack. He muttered under his breath, shaking his head.

The umpire glances at his watch and frowns. It is still twelve minutes to tea. He holds his watch to his ear, but it's still ticking. He must have misread the time before. He feels the heat well up inside his body. If he misread the time earlier, he could have misread the last ball. He tugs at his tie, envies the loose gear of the men around him. He straightens his body, takes up position hard in line with the stumps, forces his concentration from past to present. If the bowler had asked for an explanation, he would have given it, but he didn't. Mentally he shrugs.

The next ball goes for two and the stick-like batsman is batting into the sun again.

He hears a grunt. The ball flies past. The batsman stretches for it, nicks it with the bat so it shoots sideways in the direction of the fielder off side who launches himself full-length, scoops it up as it touches the ground and rolls over on his back with the ball clasped triumphantly mid-air. But the umpire is clear on this one. As clear as he can be.

He signals. Not out.

The bowler is in front of him and shorter, so he is forced to angle his gaze downwards. He feels too human, too vulnerable for this job. The irises he looks into are the colour and texture of walnut. The sweat runs freely down his leg. He can feel it soaking his right sock and he fights the temptation to look. A fly buzzes, whirls in a circle between their faces. Two fielders move towards them. A little girl screams as she rolls down the grassy embankment. The near batsman taps down the wicket.

But the bowler shrugs, gives a tight grin. Holding out his hand for the ball, he strides back to the mark.

It's harder still to concentrate with doubt nibbling at the edges of your mind. He'll call an early tea break at the end of the over. Everyone's nerves are taut with the heat. The temperature must be well over the century. The sea breeze is overdue; the peppermints hang heavy at the boundary.

The last ball of the over. The hands of his watch have not moved. He will have to worry about that later. In the meantime he prays for an uncontroversial last ball. He crouches low. Calls all his senses into the game. Hears the grunt, sees the ball flip past. Watches the stickman swipe as if in slow motion, hears the ball click but shallowly on the wood, rise into the air and fall lightly into the hands of the wicketkeeper who moves forward to stump. The batsman is out of his crease. Amazingly the batsman is out of his crease. Almost too late, he swings around, sees the line behind him, reaches back to dig his bat into the pitch behind the line. At the same time, the wicketkeeper sweeps the bales off the stumps. Or was it at the same time? The wicketkeeper was almost at the stumps before the batsman realised he was out of his crease. The umpire searches his memory for their faces, the confidence of the wicketkeeper, the shock of the batsman. Clear decision.

'Stumped. Tea break. Resume play in fifteen minutes.'

He sees the batsman look up, thinks he hears him say 'What the …' as he starts to walk towards him. He releases the hat to the bowler who walks off, slapping it against his knee as he goes.

'You were out of your crease.'

'No I bloody wasn't. My bat was there before he stumped. Where was you?'

The umpire squeezes his eyes together. The ground starts vibrating again and he resists the urge to look over his shoulder. They should all be leaving the field now, but instead he sees the fielders gather in a little knot. They are looking at him, shaking their heads, clenching their fists. Now the batting side is moving onto the field. Not just onto the field, but towards him. They are marching now, moving quickly in formation.

In the shade of the pavilion, the table is set for afternoon tea: triangular sandwiches, mountains of steaming scones, strawberry jam, cream and pots of tea.

Closer they come, an army of angry men. He starts running only to find that he has pads strapped to his legs that slow him down. Still his legs pump. But he is going nowhere fast and the men close quickly.

The sweat is in his eyes so he can no longer see. He tries to scream but there is no sound. Has his voice gone or is it his hearing? But he still has his sense of smell. He picks up the scent of strong sugary tea.

'Move away, fellas. Give him some room. Come on, give the bloke a break.'

A hand slips gently between the thirsty grass and the back of his head and the tea is wet and real.

‘WHATEVER HAPPENED TO SHIRL?’

On the first Saturday night of each spring, Herzel throws a party and by some form of jungle drum, we all turn up. Little changes, except this year everyone is smoking more, drinking more, the women's skirts bonded to their bottoms tighter than rice paper wraps. A teen finds a mic, waves it in front of her mouth, sings through her inhibitions. Somewhere a bottle smashes. A video streams fantasy onto the brick wall of an adjacent building. The air vibrates with the smash and rattle of cymbals, wooden sticks hammer on a drumhead, laughter pitches and shrills … I know the shape of that laughter. I know where it comes from, where it can lead.

A group of men and a youngster cluster around a rusting half-44-gallon drum that serves as a brazier. The glow from the fire has cast a bit of a spell on the scene in front of me; the shadowy figures merge past with present. The noise, too, has separated out, clear fragments of man-talk reach me.

'Whatever happened to Shirl? Anyone know where she is now?' The man who has just spoken is tall, dressed in t-shirt and stubbies. His name I have forgotten or maybe never knew. But his legs I remember – still covered with red-gold curling hair – exposed now just as they were on another evening, another party, a long time ago.

He looks around the group, his mouth curls. With the toe of his shoe he draws a wobbly circle in the loose dirt with a Y in the centre and dots all around: five dots surrounding a central symbol. Then he squats, uses the heel of his tinny to grind his diagram into the earth. The men look on silently, the youth's gaze darts back and forth between their faces and the drawing. From where he squats, the tall man looks up at each of the men in turn. 'Anyone remember this?'

'Jeez,' says a bearded man to no one in particular.

The kid is intrigued by the shaking heads and the mutterings of the others.

'Who is this Shirl … anyway?'

'Just a girl,' says the first man, clearing his throat. 'She was just a girl we all knew.'

Just a girl. Was that all she was? I remember Shirley, too, lying on her back in the sand. The way she laughingly offered up her wrists to the man with the red-gold hair standing above her. The shock in her husband's eyes that had come too late. His hand on her arm, 'Shirl, please. I beg of you.'

'Fuck off.' She had raised her head from the sand. 'Fuck the hell off.'

The circle of men around her silent. At first. At first, it could have been choreographed, some crude form of sexual ballet as the man on her left undid his belt, the night so quiet you could hear the whisper of the leather slide through the loops of his khaki shorts. Gently he took one of her wrists, looped the belt over to draw her arm towards him. The man on her right did the same. The insanity of her laughter as the tall man knelt down.

Someone had stepped forward, 'Hey guys. Cut that out. Settle. I said *settle.*'

But now it's the first Saturday night of spring at Herzel's place. The music thrums and the ground vibrates. A second young woman has joined the first. They take turns with the mic. They rotate their bodies in tandem. They sing and they giggle. The tall man stands to loom above his diagram, casts a glance in their direction. The empty can in his hand folds with a pop.

'Just a girl,' he had said. 'Just a girl we all knew.'

I knew Shirley, too. I knew her very well.

THE NO-NAME SILK TIE

In his eagerness to get aboard, he collided with a woman on the gangplank. They both gasped and recoiled, snapping apart like flying saucers bumping in the stratosphere. And then, recovering their balance before their manners, they raced on up the tilting plank. They would have reached the deck together had Tyler not deliberately slowed his speed.

He did so, not from any gentlemanly impulse or natural restraint, but because the brief contact and the sight of the flashing legs between heel and skirt suggested that further appraisal would be a good use of his time. Even as he hung back, he was reminding himself that this was what the cruise was all about.

Seconds later he arrived alongside her on the lobby deck. Lips curving smoothly, he held out his hand. 'Sorry. Very nearly toppled you there.'

Eyes greener than his own and cooler than a Siberian bank vault looked into his and he felt instantly and strangely uncomfortable. He started to lower his outstretched arm. 'I say, I'm sorry …' he began again.

'It's nothing. We were both careless.' He thought she almost smiled but if she did, it didn't reach her eyes. Or her voice.

He could think of nothing further to say, so he dropped his arm to his side with a slight smack and turned away.

The speaker above his head crackled and a tired recording of *Waltzing Matilda* filled the air. A rainbow of streamers lacing ship to shore tightened and snapped. Little shrieks of excitement bubbled up from the crowd. The cruise was underway.

As the ship surged and rolled towards the Heads, he let his body slump against the railings. He could feel his heart pumping faster and harder than the brief sprint warranted; it tended to do that these days, and it disturbed him to realise he'd been under any tension. After all, he hadn't worked in Sydney for many years and the last two jobs had been completed in Perth – too recently for comfort, but in practical terms a whole nation distant. Maybe it was just that he was getting too old for this sort of thing. But that last one had been a big haul created by the skilful manipulation of a decimal point, so now there was really no need for him to work again. Ever. He thought of the old man, still clocking-in at 8.45 every morning and out again at 5 every evening, and smiled to himself.

Even when I was a little kid you told me crime didn't pay, didn't you, Dad? But I wonder what you'd think if you could see me now: my Harry Seidler penthouse on the edge of the harbour, Corniche in the garage, top-of-the-range Rolex on my wrist. The secret, of course, lies not in being honest, but in not getting caught. I cracked that particular combination pretty smoothly. Wouldn't you say?

But, strangely, the one possession that gave him the most pleasure of all didn't really fit with this list of exclusivity and boastfulness – and that was his silk tie. And it did so because, quite simply, it meant he'd 'arrived'.

He smiled at his memory of the salesman's reaction when he'd asked him to remove the label.

'Cut it out?' The man's eyes had widened. 'But that's what makes these garments what they are, sir. The label.' He turned the tie over and hooked his thumb lightly under the brand name with its sweeping signage. 'This is what you pay for. This is what you buy.'

'Are you recommending that I not only spend big but advertise for free?'

While he waited for the right answer, he'd leaned against the shiny counter top only to be distracted when in his reflection he caught a glimpse of a boy halted and unbreathing in front of a stylishly dressed store window. The boy he hardly recognised, but the ache of wanting trapped halfway between the base of his throat and the middle of his chest was something he would never forget.

It was not the haughty, elegantly suited male mannequin that had stopped the boy, but the tie so casually flipped back across the model's shoulder. And, again, perhaps it was not the tie itself – brown striped with gold – that so affected him but the prestige that sprung from the signature so nonchalantly embroidered on the black label – the expensive flourish of the Pierre Cardin moniker, the careless sophistication of Paris, New York, the sensuous lure of 100% silk – all hopelessly and forever out of reach for the boy from the back of beyond.

Out of his reach back then. But not forever. While it might have taken him longer than he'd planned to get to the point where he had nothing to prove, finally it had happened just as he'd known it would. So now he wanted the tie not for the silken signature produced in some South China sweatshop, not for the cut, the cloth. He wanted it precisely because he could afford to ditch the bloody label. While the salesman swallowed and searched for scissors in the mess of the counter drawer, he had straightened up and slowly wiped his sleeve over the shiny top and its passage back into the past.

It was only a short time after this before he felt he could afford to start to build a future which included a woman more special than anyone he had ever known. It went without saying, of course, that she would be attractive and that she would satisfy him in bed, but he was looking for something more. He wanted a woman with similar interests to his own, but she'd also need to be someone capable of meeting the challenge his lifestyle demanded and someone with the power to match up to his passions for a long, long while. He was weary of moving from girlfriend to girlfriend, of forgetting their faces almost before he forgot their names and he knew what he didn't want. Just how this special woman would ensure his lifelong interest he couldn't quite imagine. He knew only that once he set his mind to something, he would be successful.

This cruise was the first step in a plan to find such a person who, even should she slip from his grasp, he would never ever forget.

And now he knew exactly where he would start. He thrust his hands into his pockets, rocked a little on his feet. What was there to lose? At least she was worth checking out.

He lost no time in starting the rumour, choosing the chummy atmosphere of the pool deck bar, seating himself beside an elderly couple.

'A talent scout,' he said in a bored sort of a way in answer to their overtures. Their mouths rounded.

'Ooh … well, and isn't that interesting,' they said together. 'We've never met a talent scout before.'

'Here, let me buy you a drink,' he said, raising a hand to block their excuses. 'No problem, I'm on expenses …' Which I am, he added to himself, winking at the sun as it spilled into the darkening sea. He worked hard that evening, buying drinks, spending money, elaborating on his tale until at last people started coming up to him and he knew that all he had to do was wait patiently.

But it was not until the third night, after dinner, that she approached him at the ship's rails. He must have looked surprised because she apologised at once for startling him. Was it really that her voice sounded softer and breathier than it had on their first encounter or was it because he wanted it so? He breathed in.

'Look. Let's start again, shall we?' he suggested gently. Remembering her original snub and smiling in such a way that it would be clear he remembered, he held out his hand once again. 'Tyler Murray's my name. My friends call me Ty.'

This time she took his hand in a crisp firm clasp, but dropped it sooner than he would have wished. 'And I'm Isabel,' she said, hesitating slightly before adding, 'Isabel Love.' She paused again. 'I heard you're a talent scout?'

He figured she was tired of wisecracks about her name, guessed too she was after a direct answer.

'Yes. Yes, I am. I work for myself. My own company, you know ...'

'Is it profitable?'

He laughed. Her punches were not exactly feather-light, but he liked her style. Smiling comfortably into her face, he pictured his offshore bank account. 'It sure is,' he said happily. 'It certainly is. I could buy this tub twice over.'

But it was not until they started talking that he found he had more in common with Isabel Love than green eyes. It turned out they both loved oysters and disliked cats. They preferred books to music and lush apartments to rickety terrace houses. They both enjoyed travel and meeting people and both thought that money was only important when you did not have enough.

'The big question then becomes: how much is enough?' he asked. She laughed, flashed her eyes, rested her hand lightly on his arm.

They spent the rest of that evening walking, talking and laughing about this and that; in fact, he felt so comfortable he was about to suggest a nightcap when she smiled a sudden goodnight and, before he could reach out, she had slipped away to talk to two of the ship's officers. He wanted to warn her that their bright white uniforms barely hid their dark intentions. He ground his teeth and flashed messages to himself. Steady on, Ty, you hardly know the woman. Take your time. It's not like you to lose a prospect by reeling in too fast. And this one could be the one. Go slow.

But there was nothing slow about this romance. Over the next days they sunbathed together, played quoits or table tennis in the afternoons and danced away the evenings. When they went ashore he bought her a necklace of seashells and on the damp sand of the beach he drew a giant heart with his big toe.

Wherever they went, it seemed to him, they came across one or other of the handsome officers, but he quelled his jealousy by reminding himself that possession was nine points of a law he didn't believe in anyway. All the same he held her hand just a little more firmly and, back on board late one afternoon, he led her to the ship's shop to buy her a gift more valuable than the string of shells.

When he picked out a necklace of pearls she tried to protest, pushing the double-strand to one side as he went to clasp it around her neck.

'No, no, you mustn't,' she insisted. 'You've spent much too much on me already. I'll be the ruin of you.'

'Plenty more where this came from,' he said lightly. And then more seriously, 'I could never spend enough to do justice to you.' And I mean it, he thought with some surprise.

More than once he felt like telling her the truth, admitting that he was a thief, not a common thief, of course, rather an exceptional one actually, but a thief nonetheless. But each time he went to confess he was met with a coolness that raised his own temperature. He knew, as only someone who lives on his intuition can clearly know, that he was more in love than she. Right now, anyway. If he told the truth at this point, he would lose her.

But sometimes he came close to mentioning his past and often, despite himself, he found himself hinting. Like the night before the cruise was due to end and they had broken away from the sloping dance-floor to go up on deck.

'Why so tense?' she had asked, gripping hard at the rail as the ship rolled. 'Is it because we're nearly home?'

'Why should returning to Sydney make me tense?' Even to his own ears, his voice sounded defensive.

'Oh, I just thought … I don't know …' She dropped her head.

Placing his hands on her shoulders, he drew her towards him.

'Perhaps I am a little wound-up,' he said. 'You see, to tell the truth, I think I'm falling for you. And yet, I feel, despite all the time we've spent together, we know so little about each other.' She was about to speak, but he squeezed her shoulders slightly. 'No, wait, let me finish. Isabel … there's more to my life than I've let on. I've done things …'

She moved restlessly, her body against his, her fingers teasing at his no-name silk tie, loosening it a little at the collar.

'Yes?' she prompted.

'You see …' he said, and paused. The tension in her one word stopped him. There was an eagerness in her tone that clashed with the casual play of her long fingers.

So he changed his mind. Instead he said carelessly, 'All I was going to say was I'm not quite the white knight you might think I am, Isabel. Sadly, I …'

'Shush,' she whispered. Resting the fingers of one hand against his lips, she trailed the other lightly down his body. 'Let's go below.' She winked. 'See how the evening works itself out.'

When he walked into the lobby on the last morning of the cruise, he saw her at the far end of the crowded room conversing with the two officers in an animated and altogether too friendly a manner. His mouth felt dry and he started to turn away. But she had already seen him and when she smiled goodbye to the men in white and walked across to him, he was relieved to see that the night's activities hadn't diluted the warmth in her eyes.

When they disembarked a short while later he knew he had to see her again. On the cool concrete of the dock he turned to face her.

'Where do we go from here?' he asked. Before she could answer, he added softly, 'I really would like to see you again.'

He kept his eyes on her face, trying to read her mood as she rummaged around in a large leather shoulder bag. But when at last she looked up, her eyes were as hard as gemstones.

'I'm afraid that's not possible,' she said and over her voice he heard the cold snap of handcuffs about his wrists. 'I'm placing you under arrest, Tyler Murray. You're wanted for embezzlement in Western Australia, two counts of armed robbery in Sydney back in 1999 and …'

With the same level of fascinated consideration that a dog will lavish on a pesky fly, he stared at her as the words fell in a jumble about his ears. He was still admiring her cool detachment when the two officers materialised, one either side of him. 'We'll take over now, Detective-Inspector Love,' he heard one say. 'Good work – and thanks.'

Smiling thinly she walked away, striding across the quayside without a backward glance, heels clicking like a cricket, her hair swinging just short of her shoulders. He shook his head and another image crowded in to replace Isabel, the men in white and the unsteady quay.

He saw his father, grey-haired and thinly erect, punching the time clock. Clocking-in and clocking-out each day, five days a week, every week of his working life.

THE VANITIES

She sees him first in the university library. Profiled against the fading reds and oranges, blues and greens of the stacks. He has a nose like the beak of an ibis, she thinks. Curved high, sharp and savage. She watches as his left hand grips the side of the metal cabinet as he swings in towards the books, his head shifting with his gaze across the shelves, the too-thin fingers of his other hand raking at his hair. They find the titles they are searching for at the same time and as they reach the check-out counter she fishtails into the space ahead of him, punches her book along the flat white of the countertop. He mutters. Slowly she turns to face him.

'Sorry?'

His eyes stare past her; his words unload. 'To push in front is not courteous. In my country –'

She tosses her head, turns her back on him, a small fire of anger flaring at the centre of her chest. She is aware of the level of his annoyance in the disturbance of his breathing as he stands behind her, aware too of the faintest trace of perfume in the air. She wants to say:

However, this is not your country. Or is it? It is not something she wishes to concern herself with. Or to think about for that matter.

But by the time she has reached the careless crowdedness of the café and settled herself at her favourite table, she has forgotten him. Surrendering to the dissonance of sight and sound that surrounds her, she sips her coffee. Beyond the pond that edges the terrace, the grounds stretch towards the arched buildings of the main university with the tall clock tower in the shadows of which two people are fencing. The roar of their challenges and the grate and ping of their foils ring out across the campus to puncture the playful chatter either side of her.

This is her space, her safe house, so she does not notice the shadow of the man as it falls across her table. His approach is suffocated by the backdrop of squealing laughter, and it is not until he pulls out a chair she sees him in front of her. The warmth rises in her body, but the face she presents is chill.

'May I.' He drops into the chair, places his two books on the table slightly to one side of hers.

'No,' she says in response to the question he has not really asked. She treasures this island feeling she has carved in the rowdy crowd, draws her paper cup towards her. 'No,' she says again. And then, in case he has not understood, she adds, 'I prefer to sit alone.'

But he is undeterred. A triangle of sun lights one of his cheeks. He is examining her carefully now, no longer avoiding her eyes, his coolness well-matched with hers. He moves his head so the light plays about his mouth, softens it. It sets him free, she thinks, changes him. In the library he had looked caged. Here on the terrace, he is looser, more open. His posture is easy and graceful; so lightly in fact does he appear to be sitting that she imagines most of his weight still on his feet. She wishes she had a smoke.

He is still watching her closely. She takes a stance within herself. Draws further in. She resents this interruption, this disturbance of her thoughts. The intrusion into her space. This is her table. The more crowded the terrace, the more concentrated her aloneness. 'No,' she repeats. But the utterance is lost. It is as though she is testing the word itself, or even the principle underneath. It is as if she is unsure of the authority it contains to remove him, unsure of her own power, of the depth and degree of her own remoteness.

But he is no longer looking at her. Instead his fingers reach out to pick up her book. She stares while he turns it over in his hands, bending forward slightly so that the spike of sun shifts again, moves up to bounce off the irises of his eyes, turning the black-brown to something lighter. As variable as layers of igneous rock, she thinks, not soft as brown eyes should be. He smiles across at her.

'Ah, Attar, my favourite. Definitely my favourite. Why Attar? May I ask what you are studying?'

She holds out her hand for the book, but he ignores the gesture. She wants to tell him to give back her book and leave her alone. Fuck off is her language. She likes being alone. She chooses aloneness. That is why she always manifests this small table beside the pillar two feet from the narrow pond. But now something stops her. Perhaps it is the way he holds the book, as if it is indeed a book – and therefore something to be valued. He almost carries the lightness of it in his hands, as if the lightness is a thing in itself, his fingers skimming the edges of the pages, slipping gently through and across.

'Do you know this story?'

'How can I? I only just checked the book out. As you saw.' She bites at the words.

He sweeps his hand, a short gesture towards her as if to move her anger backwards, to some other place behind them both. At the same time he shakes his head. Perhaps she could simply move. She glances about for another table, but the terrace is bursting with post-lecture relief, for all the world like Gino's on a Saturday morning. The only other option is to leave the terrace, but to do so is to admit defeat. However melting hot she feels inside, this she will not do.

After a moment, he speaks quietly. 'Attar lived in the twelfth century. In Persia. He was a poet. But a philosopher, too. This, his *Conference of the Birds*, is I think not only his best work, but one of the most clever works to come out of Persia which has, of course, produced many masterpieces from poet-philosophers like Rumi and Omar Khayyám, among many others.' He rubs his chin. Leaning across the scratched white plastic of the table-top, bending away from the noise into their circle of quiet, he holds the book between his hands as one might hold a prayer book. 'The story tells of many birds that assemble at the start of a spiritual search for the Simorgh.'

She pushes back her chair, goes to rise. She draws in her breath, wants to grab the book, her book. But that would cause a disruption, give the crowd an excuse to stare.

'The Simorgh is God. He lives like a king in a palace and to reach that palace, to come face to face with the Simorgh, it is for the birds a little like human souls searching for God. Do you see? These birds get together in conference to appoint one of their number, the wise Hoopoe, to lead them on the search.'

She shrugs, and for emphasis folds her arms, but she has the uncomfortable sense that it is he who is now in his element, that in moving out of the circle of her coldness into the warmth of the story, he has become as detached as she.

'Each bird is representative of a different – what can I call it – a "vanity" perhaps? And this might be greed or pride or anger or envy, something like that. And of course these characteristics or vanities hinder the birds in their search for the truth, just as they hinder us humans.'

His voice is becoming softer, more lilting, as he talks. It is as though he is listening to himself, telling the tale more for himself than for her. She senses that his gaze, too, has turned inward; he is still looking at the book in his hands, but no longer seeing.

'All sorts of tests are set for these thousands of birds that undertake the journey, just as there are tests for us in real life, and each test is described in this story as a valley. So you see: there are the valleys of love, detachment, awe, bewilderment and so on. Some birds fail the tests, some pass.'

She finishes her coffee, rests her elbows on the table.

'So, how many make it?'

'Thirty. In the end only thirty make it to the Simorgh's palace. *Si morgh* actually means thirty birds. Finally, the birds come face to face with themselves. Like a mirror, the birds look at the Simorgh and see themselves. They have passed the tests and overcome the sins of their egos. They are one with God. They *are* the Simorgh.'

He stops speaking, looks up from the book. 'In this world, we are all vanities. You, for instance. Perhaps at this point of your journey, you are fear. Fear disguised as anger.'

'And you are rude and arrogant.' She rears back. Her words hiss into the space between them and she is unpleasantly aware that the students at the nearest tables have fallen silent. The plastic cup twists and breaks in her hand. 'Just what do *you* see when you look in the mirror?'

Snagged in the smoke of their locked gaze, she thinks of the roo, that time, in the beam of the headlight, the muddy confusion in its eyes that went beyond fear. She struggles to breathe. Fighting hard against the sense that there is some sort of overlap between their circles of disquiet, she looks away and up to the ceiling where the lacy reflections of the rippling pond thump through her like king waves crashing on a rocky beach.

He snaps the book shut, spins it across the table. He gathers up his own books and when next he speaks the tone of his voice is curiously different, more stilted, the language less fluent. It is almost as if he has come back into his own body as he says, 'Enough of this lecture then. Read Attar and perhaps we talk philosophy one day.'

Silence, sniggers, a dozen pairs of eyes. She doesn't know what she wishes, knows only that he is about to leave and that she must gather herself back into her body. She senses that although she has gained a hit, he is the better fencer of the two and that the comparative calm of his riposte has done more than nick her skin. His chair scrapes the tiled floor. She tracks back. Shrugs. For the first time, his eyes waver.

'I came to say originally … What I really meant to say was to please forgive me for my comment in the library. Although I am used to your ways, I forget sometimes and it still makes me angry … makes me angry with myself when I do that. When I am preoccupied, as always I am with books, I forget.' He inclines his head and moves away, winding between the scattered groups.

She watches his back until he reaches the door, gathers more deeply into herself, hardly breathing, suffocating the little waves that churn through her body and mess with her mind, swapping the glimpse of companionship for the comforting island of self. Only as the ripples fade from the ceiling and the shadows of the tall oaks at the end of the oval stretch out towards her, only as the clamour rises again and then finally dies, does she begin to move; finds solace in the clicks as she stretches her neck, presses her back against the chair and moves her tongue around her dry mouth to start the saliva flowing.

The fencers have long since packed up and gone home. The late-afternoon sun is gilding the western face of the clock tower; the highs and lows of choral music drift towards her.

'Finished, are we.'

She starts as a hand sweeps her split cup into the debris of a loaded tray, realises the chairs about her are being stacked.

'No,' she murmurs as she picks up her book and stands to leave. 'No, not finished. Maybe just beginning.'

BITSA

As usual, it's not long before I'm spotted by a ranger. No sooner had I spied the white paddy wagon with its big blue-lettered sign, I knew it would only be seconds before it swung towards me. Sometimes I can have a bit of fun before I'm caught, so I loped along the pavement for a bit, the car keeping pace with me until I faked exhaustion and started to slow.

The ranger got out smiling fit to split his lip, one hand behind his back, the other holding a biscuit. The biscuit was tempting, I must admit, but I knew that in the other hand he held a rope and I wasn't ready to be caught. So as soon as he stretched out towards me I swung away and began to trot, quite slowly at first, but well out of reach: rope-burn is something I don't want to experience ever again. We jogged along like this by the river for some time until I judged he was just about whacked, at which point I lengthened my stride and made for a grove of paperbarks.

'I'll get you, you crazy dog. You got big trouble coming. Just you wait and see,' he yelled after me. A mistake, all that shouting, I could have told him; he didn't have the breath to waste. But his words had the uncomfortable ring of my mother's.

'You'll get yourself into trouble one of these days,' my mother had said. 'You'll learn soon enough that everything you do in life has consequences.' She nibbled delicately at the nails of her back foot as she always did when she was nervous and I know she was thinking of the night she was taken by my father. Mother was a pedigree, a Doberman, and patrician to the end of her long nose while he, on the other hand, was a Ridgeback. Mostly. Much to the annoyance of her owners who had other plans for her, my father had clambered over the wall and snuck up on her one night. Nine weeks later there were thirteen pups, some with ridges, some without.

However, you don't necessarily have to instigate consequences to be on the receiving end; sometimes you can inherit them and then it's a question of luck. I learned this right from the start when seven of my brothers and sisters were put back into the yard squealing and carrying on as they tried to bend back on themselves to lick at the bleeding stumps of what had been their tails. My mother sighed and tried to soothe them by licking and nudging them, but she was very conscious of her breed and she knew this was probably their best chance in life. The rest of us sat hard on our beautiful tails and thanked the dog god that we'd inherited the ridge from our father.

But that wasn't all I got from my father. I'd also inherited his addiction for wandering, for getting in and getting out of just about any enclosure. Or any scrape for that matter. He came to visit us most nights in the early days after we were born. We'd hear scrabbling the other side of the wall; for half a breath he perched on top and then he bounded down. First he would touch noses with my mother, nuzzle at the backs of her ears, take a quick look at us with his chest expanded almost to bursting, before he was gone quick as he came. I couldn't wait to be big enough to clamber up that wall.

The problem was the very first time I was successful I felt so exhilarated that nothing could stop me doing it again and again. And it's continued the way it started, this habit of mine. I'm no sooner with a new owner than I prowl the boundary to check the gate and fences – and I reckon I now have the wit and the knowledge to get out of just about any enclosure. That's powerful stuff that keeps me coming back for more. The downside is that I've slept on the cold floors of more city pounds than any dog alive – with a further consequence being that I've had many owners. It's only been by experiment that I've found out how to attract the people who will do the job of owning a dog well, and how to discourage those who obviously won't.

You can tell most things about people from the houses they live in, so last time I found myself loose I thought I'd choose my new owner by picking the house. Those facing the river were mostly two and three-storey dwellings with the remote look about them that meant I'd be spending a lot of my time in a backyard which was really only an expensive and lonelier version of a Council pound. Others had their gardens – grass, hedges, trees – almost strangled to death by too much clipping so I knew without meeting them that those owners were control freaks. That's bad news for a dog like me. Another had concrete around the house which showed they didn't want to be bothered with anything beyond their immediate selves, let alone a dog. And then there was the one with a tricycle abandoned in the middle of the driveway. Toddlers I didn't need, not after the last had poked her finger in my ear, which was nice, and then in my eye, which wasn't.

So the house I chose that last time was long and low and white with a red roof and wide verandahs all round. The verandahs meant sun in winter, shade in summer and it had a gate so there would be no issues keeping me in. Or so they would think. I lay in the middle of the driveway, my nose between my paws, and waited, part of me watchful for a reappearance of the white van.

The first person home was a boy, very thin and tall and freckled, with a weighty satchel on his back and his head bent so low to compensate that I thought he was going to walk right into me. I sat up, wagged my tail, so he started back.

'Oh my God,' he said. 'Where did *you* spring from?'

I looked into his eyes and whined, and after a minute he shrugged off his satchel and bent down to offer me his hand to sniff. When he scratched behind my ears, I dropped my head and panted because I couldn't help myself. I knew, easy as that, we had a match.

'You have a collar, but no tag, so what've you been up to, eh? What are we going to do with you? Looks like you need a drink. Come on home, we'll see what the parents think.'

I could have told him exactly what his parents would think and how they'd react, but that was something we had to go through.

'Keep him?' His mother frowned and put her hands on her hips when she got home to find me there. By that time, I was sitting in the middle of the lounge carpet with a posture that would have made my own mother proud. My gaze travelled from one to the other as they argued. 'Are you mad, Lee? An animal that size costs a fortune to feed. Besides it's stealing. You can't just keep a dog you've picked up. He obviously belongs to someone.'

'I didn't pick him, he picked me. He's lost. We could advertise. See if someone comes to claim him. Besides you promised. Remember …'

She squirmed a little, but she had an answer. Mothers do.

'Yes, but don't you want to choose one – well, from a breeder? Choose exactly what you want, instead of – a bitser?' Disparaging though the description was, I'd had worse, and I could see her gaze on my ridge, so I shifted around so she could see the full perfection of it. 'Though it looks like he's got a fair dollop of ridgeback. Like my first dog.' The glare in her eyes softened just a touch. 'Stubborn, that one certainly was, but loyal …' She sighed. 'He'd have laid down his life for me, that dog.' She shook her head and I could see it was something from the past talking through her when she said, 'All right. Just for the moment. Can't turn him out in the dark anyway. Put notices up in the park and in the deli. And put an ad in the local paper. You'd better call the pound, too, in case his owners are frantic.' She looked her son right in the eye. 'And Lee. Get this, will you. He's not permanent, so don't go getting fond of him.'

But I *was* permanent, well, as much as I'd been anywhere. Although I did my usual checking of the boundaries, just in case, for the first time my heart wasn't in it. And I had a feeling my last owners wouldn't rush to claim me.

'Bitser, she called you,' he said when he put me to bed that first night on a thick rug in a corner of the laundry. 'Damned cheek.'

But the name stuck and that's what he called me from then on – except when he pronounced it, it sounded much softer. And, as I predicted, no one came to claim me, so after a short time, my new family registered me and attached a bright green tag to my collar.

It was obvious Lee knew something about dogs, but he had a lot to learn about me and I could see he was nervous the first time he took me for a walk.

'I wonder whether you're a fighter,' he said, tightening his fingers on my lead as an oversize German Shepherd shambled towards us. But to tell the truth, fighting's something I've never been much interested in – there's a deal too much pain and effort involved – so when I didn't react even after the other dog quickened its stride and growled, I could see he was impressed.

My first time off the lead was interesting, too.

'For heaven's sake, don't run off,' he said, letting off the clip, his muscles twitching, ready to move as if he expected me to bolt up the road – as if he could have caught me if I had. But when I continued to stand alongside him, he scratched his head. 'Well, don't you want to sniff around then?' But I was more interested in showing him what I could do, so I just stood there looking straight ahead, ignoring the two yapping bundles of fluff that passed, and waiting for Lee to make a move.

'Okay, let's go,' he said and from that time on he didn't bother with the lead. Sometimes he would test me. He knew my fondness for hard biscuit and he would place one on the pavement and then walk off with me and wait for a dog to come by and pick it up. That was one of the hardest tests, but my mother would have been proud of the disdain I mustered as we watched from a little way off as one dog or another stumbled across the treat and settled to chew it despite the tugging on their collars by their owners. I knew, in any case, there were more where those came from. And in some strange way that I'm unable to fathom, the trust and the pride he had in me more than made up for watching an ill-behaved mutt slavering over what by rights was mine.

But one day I saw the white van with the sign before he did and knew before it rolled up alongside that the driver was none other than the ranger who had threatened me when I first came to the area.

Lee moved to clip on my lead too late, so he stood with his fingers tucked around my collar instead.

'You aware this is a leads-only area, mate?' The ranger spoke to Lee, but his gaze was on me and I could see he was trying to recollect where he'd seen me before.

'Yes, sir.'

'Well then. Why isn't your dog on a lead?'

'He's a good dog, this one. He doesn't need a lead. Let me show you …'

'The law doesn't recognise any difference between good dogs and bad dogs.'

'In that case, the law's an ass,' said Lee, surprising himself, I think, that the words came out so easily.

I'd heard his father say just that the night before, but his father had been half-joking and I didn't have to be a dog to sense the ranger wasn't big on jokes. We watched as his phony smile disappeared. His neck took on a rosy sheen and there was warning in his eyes. I tensed, too, getting ready to growl; it was only the confidence in the knuckles that rested on my withers that kept me quiet.

'Don't get smart with me, buster,' the ranger snapped, watching my hackles that were rising with a will of their own. 'Just so's you know: the fine's $100 which'd make a bit of a dent in your pocket money. I'll let you off this time. Take it as a warning. But don't let me see that animal off the lead again. Ever. Clear? And, for good measure, give me your name, address and phone number.'

'Yes, sir.' His hand trembling on my collar, Lee stammered his address and clipped on the lead.

Since the ranger often trawled that stretch of popular parkland, from that day on we walked sedately joined together by the lead from the house to where the pavement became track before disappearing into river scrubland.

And then Lee would free us up to play all sorts of games like my tracking him down while he pretended to hide or finding a biscuit buried under a foot of soil or we'd take turns chasing each other until I could tell he'd had enough.

At night, I'd curl up at his feet while he did his homework and from time to time he'd bend down to scratch my ears like he did when we first met.

But it was the days that were long, lying with my head on my paws waiting for him to come home. If I had only known then what would happen later, that time would have been trivial. But that's the thing about consequences: they don't always announce themselves ahead of time. One day the old obsession started to move restlessly in me until it got so strong I had to test myself.

The limestone wall that enclosed this property was high; nothing that I hadn't tackled successfully before, but I hadn't jumped for quite some time now. It was about time for Lee to return from school and I had in mind that I would surprise him by going to meet him. I ran at the wall a few times just to limber up, to remind my muscles of the spring that was needed to run up the wall to the top and the control required to balance long enough to drop down the other side. As it turned out, it was the perfect jump.

I'm a lucky dog. I had always been a lucky dog. But this time they had a net.

'I warned him,' said the ranger to his colleague and I knew from the way he looked at me with his tongue sitting pink on his bottom lip that he remembered me from before. No sense in fighting them, so I jumped straight up into the van when they opened the door. If I'm to be honest, there was a shade of excitement in being caught again, a sense of thrill which started at the tip of my tail. Besides, I was pretty sure that I wouldn't have long to wait before Lee came to claim me.

As it turned out, I was wrong. The concrete was colder than I remembered and I didn't have much appetite for the biscuits they shoved in the cell before dark. I hadn't counted on spending too much time here and it was a dark night. No moon, no light at all up there, but that didn't stop the rest of the pack howling. It was hard not to think of my comfy rug back home. Right now I'd be tucked into a ball waiting for my night-time snack.

But there was something out there in the dark, the other side of the diamond-mesh fence. Nothing I could hear for the racket the others were making. But a scent? A scent I recognised. Slowly my tail started to wag. I got to my feet and, protected both by the noise and the black night, slunk down the length of the run to the fence at the far end.

'Bitsa?' Lee whispered, sticking his fingers through the mesh, scratching between my eyes. 'What've you gotten up to now, you silly dog? I've been looking for you all over the place.' I could see he was cross and scared and trying to be neither. 'You can't spend the night here. I've tried phoning. I couldn't raise them. What can we do?'

His eyes flicked back and forth looking for a way to get in; I saw him spy a gate and then his disappointment when he realised it was padlocked. But then his gaze travelled from the gate to the top of the high fence and in that instant I knew exactly what he was planning to do.

As he kicked off his shoes, I began to bark. The other dogs understood; almost instantly the desolate howling changed to something decidedly more purposeful and they all rushed to the end of their runs. We had such a level of understanding between us, I knew that if I could only get his attention, get him to return his focus to me, I could stop him.

Because what he didn't know was that there was a live strand of wire that ran along the top of that fence. In the dark, he couldn't see the little triangular sign they always fix on fences like this. He didn't have my breadth of experience with enclosures, hadn't seen a cat react to the volts going through its body as I had. Like most dogs, I'm not fond of cats and their taunting habits, but it's ugly when it happens that way.

But for the first time I couldn't reach Lee. This boy with whom I could communicate by look alone was no longer listening to me, but to a voice deep within himself. His mouth was set in a thin line and his body was trembling with something stronger than fury.

'Bastard,' he muttered. 'He had it in for you from the first, didn't he, fella. He knows where I live. He could have called. He could have called me.' His face glowed through the dark. His fingers and toes curled into the diamonds of wire and he started to climb.

All of a sudden the lights snapped on with a glare that made a mockery of the night; there were shouts and the thump of running feet. Two men were pounding across the yard towards him, but Lee was moving up that fence so fast, they wouldn't get to him in time.

His foot was almost out of reach. There was only one thing to do. Settling back on my haunches for the leap of my life, I sprang just as he reached for the top strand.

THE DEADLY GERM OF DOUBT

Being no longer young and therefore quite familiar with frustration in one form or another, the writer knew the concealed danger of doubt only too well. What might start small and contained – no more, perhaps, than a momentary hesitation over a comma – had the potential to spread, to cast a growing uncertainty over the phrase, the sentence and the paragraph until it hung, heavy and brooding, over the entire work. From there, he suspected that like any virus it could multiply and divide until, finally, it turned back to feast upon the host body.

There was nowhere to go with thoughts of this nature so when for the fourth or fifth day in a row, the words refused to spark as he knew they could and the bills started mounting in his mind faster than they were gathering on the hall table, the writer looked out over the low wall of the verandah and saw the enemy as the drought.

While this was inaccurate, it's true that the heat felt like a mighty animal – or given its power, like a god perhaps – in the way it filled the space between the baking red-dirt and the high and useless cloud. It puffed and stretched so the air he breathed burned his throat even while it condensed on his body. It turned into salty droplets that ran into his eyes and fell onto the keyboard until he wondered whether it might be possible to be electrocuted by the literal sweat of his own brow.

He shivered. Only the flies had energy, whirring in like fighter planes to suck and sting, before spiralling upwards for a ride on the mucky fan above his head.

It was the sort of day that made him wonder whether it might be wiser to give up. Give in his notice, pack up the few possessions he had and move back down south – to the coast perhaps – and get a job. A real job. Or what passed for a real job in the real world.

Nine months back, when he had come across the small advertisement, it had all the signs of providing exactly the right solution at the right time. Serendipitous was the word that came to mind given he was looking for a quiet space in which to write, preferably in the northern cattle country because that's where his next novel was to be set, and the absentee owner of this station was looking for a co-manager, for someone to do the books, pay the bills and generally look after the homestead. It would not be necessary to know anything about livestock because his colleague happened to be a stockman who knew cattle like he knew his own country.

The place itself suited him all right, the accounts and care-taking presented no difficulty, and he worked in well with the guy who was in charge of the working side of things. But that's where it stopped. Beaten for want of a wet season that never came, there was no denying that the station was in trouble. Iron-rich the sodding dirt of the Pilbara might be, but iron wouldn't fill the dams any more than it would feed the cattle. They had been trucking feed to the stock for some time already and at this rate he was unsure how long the property could remain viable.

Since he was neither the owner, nor able to seed the clouds, it was not his problem on the one hand, but on the other it was, because he'd come across this germ of doubt before. It might start in one place, but it had the potential to cast a spell of uneasiness over everything, and for some time now the book itself had stalled. Weeks had gone by – maybe months – with little to show for it. A grudging paragraph sometimes at the end of a morning's work. More at night with the cogs of his mind well-lubricated, at which point he judged he had done a good day's work until he read it through the next morning.

Blame the heat, but once the possibility of failure had lodged in his mind, he knew it had the power to swell and spread until it not only stopped him moving forward, but would nibble away at the present or even drop into reverse, so in the end there would be nothing left. Not even his life. Because once his world of words was gone, what would be left? No more, he suspected, than a broken dream.

He forced his gaze away from the smaller paddocks that stretched out in front of him towards the dry grassland. The backlighting on his brand-new laptop had switched off and for what seemed the thirtieth time that day he sighed and swept the mouse across the dust of his desk willing himself back to a time when his characters had hijacked his mind, the many times a fragment of an idea had evolved into a full-scale story with him just tapping the essence into the machine.

The metal of the computer felt cold in his hands, countering the heat, so that for several minutes he worked, writing a few words, deleting, adding. He was up to the part in his story where the station had to be auctioned to cover the owner's bad debt. The stock was to be sold, the equipment and homestead furniture repossessed. It was at this critical point that the story had locked up.

'Live, damn you, live!' he screamed. He slammed his fist down with such force that an empty beer can spun off the table, ricocheting off the opposite wall so the red-gold kelpie dreaming peacefully on the cool of the verandah was on its feet snarling before the can had stopped its roll.

But he didn't notice the dog, only that the words had disappeared from the screen and with them – just as suddenly – his anger, which was replaced by something quite opposite, something that had him speaking softly to the computer, gentling it, as if it were scared and living.

Too late now to try to recollect when he had last bothered to save his work to an external disc; the extra precaution hadn't seemed necessary. It never is, he thought bitterly, until it's too late.

'Easy does it. Steady, old girl. I hadn't backed up, you know. Don't you dare lose this week's torture ...'

But this problem was a physical thing. This was, after all, only a computer. This was something he could solve, unlike the weather pattern, unlike the insidious block. And when the machine failed to reboot, it gave him a reason to rise from the table to hunt for the start-up discs that had come glued to the back of the manual which might as well have been blank for all the use it had been. And because nothing was ever where it was supposed to be, this took some time.

Finally he found the disc and slid it in until it gave a satisfying click. He sat scarcely breathing. Singing softly, the computer completed its internal checks, the instructions appearing intermittently until at last the command he was waiting for popped up: PRESS ENTER TO ACCESS STORY.

Good. He blew out his breath in small, separate puffs, sent a prayer of thanks to the cloudy skyscape. And then he looked more closely. There was something different up there. Was it that the clouds were losing their too-bright glare and darkening just a little around the edges or was it just that his imagination had returned? He breathed in deeply. Once the rains came, the lock on his words would dissolve. He knew it. He just knew it.

Or would it? Could it be as simple as that? His hand hovered over the ENTER key. He pressed and in the time it took the software to make the adjustment, he was part of his story.

Jim sensed the flex in the weather's mood from inside the enormous workshop where he was on his back under the tractor fixing an oil leak. This was good news. Good news for the cattle. Good for everyone.

In an instant he had shrugged free of the undercarriage and was out in the open squinting up at the sky. He frowned. The clouds were boiling black, changing places with such speed he knew there must be one hell of a movement going on up there.

As he reached the house, the wind gusted down. It caught at the stack of single pages piled beside the computer, whipped the sheets off the table. But it wasn't that so much that stopped Jim at the bottom of the steps. He was a strong man in mind and body and not given to fanciful thoughts, but he didn't like what he had just seen. It was the work of a willy-willy, the way the papers twisted into a rising column before scattering. That chap should put something heavy on that pile; even a stone would do. And where was he anyway? Only Dingo Dog was here, swinging his tail, instead of panting the way he usually greeted him with his eyes half-closed.

Shaking his head, he bent to pick up the sheets of paper, laying them neatly on the table beside the open laptop, weighing them down with a half-brick. Telling his stories and the stories of his people was something that he, too, would do someday. He had more than half a lifetime of stories in him that should be passed on to his children and his children's children. Writing them down was not part of his plan because he knew the best stories were the ones that were told. That way the young fellas knew them for what they really were, something living that came from the living; they could see his face and hear his voice to judge the truth of it all which would stay with them for longer than marks on paper or a story that started out as keystrokes on a machine.

But this computer, although he would not use it for stories, he liked. He already knew how to use it, had had his first lessons in exchange for passing on some of his station know-how to the other manager bloke.

Gently he touched a key so that light and colour flashed onto the screen. Press ESCAPE TO EXIT sounded dull and not at all what he wanted so he pressed the space bar instead.

The computer obliged with another message: PRESS ENTER TO ACCESS STORY. He passed his tongue over his lips, hesitated just a moment, and then lightly pressed the key.

Dingo Dog held his head first on one side and then the other. He had been watching the computer closely all afternoon, ever since the empty tin had shocked him awake. The day had continued with surprises. First his master had disappeared and now Jim was gone, too. He would not know until mealtime whether all this was a good or bad thing, but it was clear that something strange was going on. He stretched now and padded closer.

The scent of his master's hands was all over the dark metal of the device and now on two of the keys he smelled tractor oil. He pressed with his nose to get closer to the source of the scent and the screen lit up suddenly. He jumped back, the fur rising on his neck. A slow growl started at the back of his throat, but even while he hung back every muscle of his body strained towards the thing. When a minute passed and nothing happened, he leaned forward to sniff harder at the second key.

Word got around that strange things had been happening on Mooroolbark Station. It appeared that the two managers had gone walkabout. It seemed that they had just upped and left the place just as it was. Even the dog was gone.

When it was certain that Mooroolbark had been deserted and the agent's attempts to contact the overseas owner of the heavily mortgaged property had failed, a decent period of indecision followed until the creditors started to do what creditors are paid to do. Finally the agent was left with no choice but to put the station up for auction. Over the next couple of weeks, a series of different trucks came around to collect, first, the cattle, followed by the machinery and then the contents of the old homestead.

'Funny thing, this business,' remarked one of the men who had come to take away the furniture. He stroked his beard. 'The whole place still ticking over, just like they disappeared into thin air. Nothing locked up, put away.'

He strode out onto the verandah where an open laptop sat beside a pile of paper with a brick on the top, whistled as he bent to touch the computer.

'Hey, Pete, look what we have here, mate. Just come out here and look at this will you. An almost spanking-new piece of equipment just going begging. All covered in dust. Won't do it much good.'

Pete appeared through the French doors.

'Aw, come on Alf. Leave it alone. I don't like this joint. It gives me the shits.'

But the man called Alf had his gaze fixed on the computer. 'A lovely laptop, just going to waste,' he crooned. 'Tell you what ...' Swiftly he snapped the screen shut and jerked the plug from the socket. 'After all. Gotta be some perks to this game.'

He stooped to pick up the computer from the table. 'That writer bloke's probably got his whole blinking book on this. You never know – he might come back some day and want to find his story waiting for him.'

He swung the light machine to and fro before tucking it under his arm. 'Actually, to tell the truth, I've always fancied myself a bit of a writer,' he said. 'I've a germ of an idea for a story and I might just have a go.' When the other man said nothing, he added with a laugh. 'Or if he left his story behind, how about I do the right thing and finish it off for him? How's about that, eh?'

Pete grunted and turned to go back into the house. 'Come on, let's get a move on. From the look of that sky, those clouds are getting ready to dump again.'

'Hankering for the cool of the cab, more like, you wuss.' Alf yelled after him.

He was about to follow when he stopped, wondering in that split of a moment whether the computer was worth nicking after all. Hadn't known Pete that long, had he? He might just be the type who'd dob him in.

And come to think of it, there *was* something a bit spooky about the place. Sort of lifeless. That is, apart from this computer which, he had just realised, was fairly pulsing, the vibrations travelling right up his arm. Staring down at the machine, he ruffled his hair, starting at the icy touch of his own hand on his forehead and gazing then at his fingers – quite absently at first – before wondering at how cold they were, how grey the skin. The dust? It must be all this dust. That was before he looked about him and saw the dirt up here was red. Blood red.

Perhaps Pete was right. Maybe it would be better to leave the thing alone after all. Holding the laptop well away from his body, he moved towards the table.

ENDLESSLY ROCKING

She stares at me just as she did from the incubator nearly twenty years ago and the emotions that stir in me now are disturbingly similar to the way I felt back then. I still want to hold her, cuddle away the difficulties. But I can't. I can't any more today than I could yesterday.

Well, she demands now. Looking up at me from her Buddha stance on the carpet. *Well, what do you think?* She doesn't really want to know. What she wants is for my truths to line up neatly with hers. I can see the brightness of her mind at work in the intensity of her gaze, the working of her brain showing clearly behind her broad forehead.

But how can she know that my own mind is not there for the touching? That my thoughts have reached back into the past tense of our lives? That instead of the emerging loveliness of the young woman sitting cross-legged before me, I see a pink-and-white baby, swaddled and still but for the stern sweep of her china-blue eyes? How can she know that on the morning after her birth I stood my side of the glass wall of the intensive care unit, my gaze crossing and re-crossing along the lines of humidicribs, frantic to recognise my own child? How can she know the pride I felt – and the special burn of the tears that flowed from that pride – when my gaze returned again and again to the pink-and-white babe two rows back from the plate-glass window.

It was two days before they brought her out from behind her sealed plastic crib, two long days before they let me hold her. How can she know that in our mutual eagerness we made a mess of our first joint project? That they advised me not to persist with breastfeeding, but to offer her bottled milk instead? Which produced the first guilt of the many that followed? How can she know any of this if I don't tell her?

I haven't answered her question because I am caught in this sticky trap of the past, unable for the moment to speak. She is looking at me, into me, trying to understand, I think. But I know that on the outside my face shows nothing. That my smile hides the stirring confusion inside me. It has always been so. My wanting to tell her and my inability to do so. My wanting to hug away the gap between us, to bring out the truths from my mother soul and lay them in front of her, so she can see how it was. So she can see that the hurt wasn't hurt for hurt's sake, but human souls caught up in the confusion of their searching.

I find I'm rubbing one leg against the other. A mother mantis. Muttering. To anchor my mind, I take the lid off the little china teapot and stir. The tea-leaves whirl, dip and settle. Answers? Perhaps that's where I should look for answers.

She sighs. Looks away. *Come here*, she orders her kitten. It runs to her, drops, coils in the triangle of her lap. Her hair falls over her eyes as she bends to it, stroking, almost purring herself, lips apart. When the kitten moves suddenly, springing at the white penguin insignia embroidered on the pocket of her shirt, she catches its ginger paws, laughing. Her hands are dimpled still, and soft, the only outside sign she is still half-child. The kitten springs again, hooks its claws into the penguin. This time she frowns. *No*. She is stern and the animal stops its pugilism, settles and sleeps instantly. Secure. She will make a good mother. An ordinary mother. That is what she wants to be. That is what she wanted of me. The tea is hot and burns my lips.

Ever since she was a toddler she has loved babies. She holds and soothes the infants of her young friends with the artless confidence of a clinic sister. She has that gift. There is a firmness in her, a knowledge of being right that relaxes her and which, in turn, relaxes them. The kitten obeys her. Her children will do the same. She will rule firmly but with love. Yes, she will be a good mother. Perhaps for her it will come naturally.

Despite the air conditioner, the sun's heat slants with summer-end harshness through the thin fabric of the blue curtains and my mind slides backwards again. I see her four, maybe five years ago in the austere corridor of her boarding school, fingers digging into her hips, eyes smoking blue-white.

I don't know why you can't be an ordinary mother, she had hissed. *Why can't you just be an ordinary mother like everyone else's?*

I snapped back, *What's an ordinary mother? What do you mean?*

But I knew, of course. An ordinary mother doesn't work, doesn't rear her children in the office, doesn't travel, divorce, remarry, travel, study, work harder and get herself widowed. An ordinary mother isn't forever distracted. Instead, an ordinary mother bakes (cakes), is confident and capable, serves on the Parents and Citizens Committee and spends all her spare time with her children. Not just the quality time I and my Spockian work peers tried unsuccessfully to dilute our guilt with. An ordinary mother handles her own children and the children of her friends with a self-assurance that is innate not learned. Yes, I know what an ordinary mother is. But it's nothing to do with loving. Or caring.

Mother! You didn't hear what I just said!

Her voice is hot at the edges, but she's smiling. My concentration returns to the room she's decorating so confidently; the old rocker has been re-upholstered and the curtains have been hung, one hemmed; the other's threads are a kitten's paradise. Maybe it has happened so often, this attempt on her part to communicate with a distracted mother that she doesn't care anymore. Doesn't feel it or doesn't take it as a hurt.

I am hurting though, because I don't know how to make amends for the years when I could have been an ordinary mother. A fierceness of feeling jabs at me. I want to say, I'm sorry, I'm sorry. Tell me how I could have done it better. Where did I go wrong? Or is it too late? Too late to rewrite the texts of all our lives? That is what I want to say. But the years of not saying still hold me back.

She rises suddenly – all her movements are sudden – and drops the kitten in my lap as she leaves the room. The kitten is as unprepared as me; the sharp tips of its claws pierce the denim of my jeans. I breathe in and feel the skin around my eyes tighten.

When she returns a few minutes later, there's another rush of pain as the kitten gathers itself to spring, runs to her, plays thread-the-needle in and out her legs.

As she stands in front of me, I know it's time to look at my watch. *I have to go. Thanks for the tea. That was lovely.* She says nothing and I make thank-you sounds to still the buzzing of the silence.

And then she asks, *Do you still want the sewing machine?* I nod and we carry it between us down the steps and out into the street where my car is parked.

We've left the door open. The kitten? Will it be all right? It won't run away? Casually I say this. It's her house. Her home. I have no right to nag. She is learning to be a woman, to have her own worries. My opportunity to nag is past.

But for the first time I see concern on her face. She drops her side of the case to the verge and her eyes turn transparent. She steps back quickly.

Oh no no ... I forgot ... I have to fly ... see you Mum ... and thanks for coming.

A wave and she is gone behind the big wall. I stand for a long time looking at that wall. It is built of burnt red brick, high because of the traffic, curving back in towards the house at one end. Tucked into the curve, there is a gate. I lean back against the heat of the car, like a boxer on the ropes. I parry the feelings that spring at me from that wall. I wish, aloud, for the courage to say what I always intend to say, but my voice does not sound like my own.

I gaze at the gate. Just a few short steps. Just, *Thank you for being you*. That's all it would take. A start. I can build from there.

The sweat starts popping out on the insides of my wrists, damp between my breasts. I move towards the gate and in the fierceness of my focus stumble over the sewing machine. I had forgotten about the machine. Forgotten about time, too. I look at my watch. But my mind is fuzzy and I see but cannot read the hands. I know I have to get the machine into the car. My hands and fingers work to open the back of the hatch, to pick up and heft the heavy case over the lip of the boot. I bang the lid and start for the gate.

As I work to free the bolt, I hear her on the phone. Her words are clear and light, riding high towards me on a sudden short breeze.

Yes, she is saying, *Yes yes yes, I'd love to. When? Tell me when. I'd just love to go*. Her voice is warm and happy, the words breaking up with laughter. I stand with my hand on the ugly bolt, sweat condensing on my forehead.

The day is hot. My blood beats. I feel a longing that matches the longing I felt outside that wall of glass so long ago. I still want to hold her. Then it was the outside world that stopped me from stepping in; now I am stopped from the inside.

But whose hurting is it that I now want to cuddle away? What unsubtle change has been wrought by time?

Slowly, I take my hand from the gate and turn back to the car.

That day, the sun burns into my brain. My mouth is full of salt.

The years roll on, make overlapping rings around us both. But the sound of the cradle rocking still slap-slaps at the edges of my dreams.

THE SCHOOLTEACHER

The scene before the teacher is one of battle, the clamour so high that he reaches the desk at the front of the class unnoticed. The two sexes are divided, strung out along the sides of the room. They are using paper darts and ruler-propelled rubber erasers for ammunition, books as shields, desks as sandbags. The gap between the forces is closing as the rubbery feet of the desks shudder along the vinyl floor tiles.

The boys are gaining on the girls. Flushed faces swing towards the teacher, observe his apparent lack of concern, swing back to face the enemy. This is the first day of their final school year.

The teacher appears undisturbed. Only slightly interested, in fact. But the look on his face is one of reflection, not boredom. He is standing with his head held slightly to one side, fingers lightly clasped. He is not a young man, but neither is he old. The clue to his age comes from his forehead which is wider and higher than it would be if it were fashioned by wisdom alone.

The minutes pass slowly, and it is only when they sense that perhaps he intends to stand in front of them, silent, for the full forty-five minutes of their first Lit lesson, that the students collapse into a grudging quiet.

Desks are swung back to face the front of the room and the rowdy class, apart from the occasional outbreak of crudely muted laughter, switches to silence.

When he continues to stand – still, but for his eyes that flicker back and forth to learn their faces – they become confused, restless again. One young man, bolder than the rest (safer, too, seated as he is at the back of the room) pulls hard on a thick elastic band, sends a rubber missile flipping through the air to strike the neck of the owner of the short white shift three rows in front of him. Whether this is the target he intended is unclear. Exposing long clean legs of basted brown, she rises to retaliate, decides instead to ignore it and slumps back, sulking.

Into the silence, the teacher speaks. Perhaps he thinks they know each other well enough by now because this is not the usual introduction. Instead he speaks in a voice so quiet they are forced to lean towards him.

'I have only two rules,' he says. 'And those rules are, firstly, that during the year and in addition to the recommended reading, you each carry a novel around with you – in your schoolbag, in your pocket or wherever you can get at it easily – to enjoy whenever you have a spare minute. It's important, of course, that it's something you enjoy reading. Imperative in fact.' His eyes linger on their faces. 'The second …'

He is interrupted by the disconcerting sound of rubber on vinyl. The girl in white has thrust her desk forward. She raises her hand to flag him sullenly.

He stops, nods: 'Yes?'

The class waits. The girl's eyes are held wide. But the innocence they project clashes with the way she holds herself. The two signals are opposite, but he does not dare to look too closely. His business is to teach.

'Can it be about *anything*?' Her voice is light with only a hint of tease. 'So long as it's something we enjoy reading, can the book be about anything? Anything at all?' Anticipating, the class buzzes, sways delightedly.

He nods. 'I'll answer that question by telling you my second rule,' he says. 'And that is that the book has to be one the school would approve of.'

The disappointment is loud. Words clatter on words, groans on groans. Desktops bump, jump. The students make their displeasure known. All but for the girl. She hasn't yet finished. Her lip curls. There is another hush like the last. The air starts to pump.

'Does that mean that it can't contain any …?' She stops and looks down, moistens her lower lip, crosses her legs at the ankles.

The collective gaze of the class swirls from the girl to the teacher.

'Any? Any what?' He raises one eyebrow.

She rubs her knees together, shrugs. 'You know what I mean.' She slaps her notepad shut. This is more than the class could have hoped for and their gaze slews from one to the other like spectators at a tennis match.

'No. No, I don't.'

She takes a breath, leans into the back of her chair and says boldly. 'Well … do you mean no sex?'

He has a puzzled look on his face. 'Sex?' he asks. 'Sex? What's that?' The class claps and cheers.

In winning the round he has chanced her antagonism, but instead she seems pleased. She opens a text titled *The New Maths* and, ignoring the hullabaloo around her, affects instant engagement.

A few weeks into the semester he has come to know her and her challenges. Of all his classes, he looks forward to this the most and he has the pleasant, though untested, feeling that she does the same.

They pass each other out of class one day at the corner of the quad, she going one way, he another. But she stops because she has something to show him.

'*Love Story* by Eric Segal.' She flashes the book in front of him. 'Have you read it?' Her fair hair is caught back in a knot and her face with its high cheekbones is soft and clear. He is aware she is watching him just as closely.

'No,' he admits. 'No, I haven't. I should have, but I haven't. Are you lending it to me?'

But as he reaches out to take the book, she snatches her hand back. She shakes her head. 'No, no, this is mine. You buy your own. Why don't you buy one and read it over the weekend?'

That weekend, he treats himself to a brief break on the island where on the balcony of his villa he reads the book. The following day, he reads it a second time. By the time he finishes, day is turning into night and the big red ball of sun, squatting misshapen at the edge of the world, is being sucked slowly into the sea.

He listens to the yachts making music in the evening breeze, to the crows and seagulls having their last arguments of the day. He watches the people below, talking, laughing, strolling, all in sets of twos and threes. He leans back in the orange-and-red striped canvas chair, his hands moving lightly over the cover of the book.

Staring back at the mainland, he remembers the girl, the way her toenail polish shows off her summer sandals. He guesses at the soft and hard of her young body, the length of her brown legs. On the beach below, a lone gull screams as the dark moves in.

On Monday, the teacher takes a few minutes longer than usual to pack up after class, gives her time to approach.

'Well,' she says, 'did you read it?' She twists a little on one foot.

He nods. 'I did.'

'Well?' When he doesn't answer immediately, she sucks in her breath. 'Well, what did you think? So sad. Sad, isn't it?' She pauses, looks at him closely and when he still says nothing she continues more slowly, thoughtfully. 'But happy, too, in a sort of way. In that they're not shut off from each other …'

'Shut off?'

'Oh, you know, shut off. Out of touch. With their feelings.'

'I enjoyed the book,' he says. 'Thank you for recommending I read it.'

'Enjoyed? You *enjoyed* it?'

He sees she is confused. 'Well, isn't that why you suggested I read it? For enjoyment?'

'No, not for enjoyment. Not for that reason.' This is the longest conversation they have had and she is aware she is exposing more than her legs. Her lashes drop to cover her eyes, to cover her disappointment. At sixteen, it's uncool to show you care.

She breathes in and out through her mouth, tosses her head and half-turns from him. As she leaves, she looks back over her shoulder. Curious, she asks: 'Tell me, did you cry?'

His hands have been moving busily about his books and papers. He stops, raises his head, blue eyes probe blue.

'That …' he says, 'that, my dear, you will never know.'

Her cheeks fill with colour and she continues to look at him intently. 'You're a sad case,' she says finally.

But he is gazing out through the doorway, through to the glare outside, to some distant place she cannot see and he gives no indication of having heard her. The room is filling with the next class.

She shrugs suddenly, straightens her shoulders, walks fast into the rectangle of glare.

There is a battle shaping in the neighbouring classroom. The students are waiting for their teacher, who is late, and while they wait the young men and women are at war. Erasers and paper darts swing through the air, desk lids bump and jump.

SINGAPORE STING

or

THE PARTICULAR REVENGE OF LIM WEE KIAT

Lim Wee Kiat was a busy man. It was the first day of the month and time, once again, to claim his allowance from each of his seven sons and three daughters. His children were widely scattered over the island and since he had to call on them personally to collect or to remind them, gently of course, of their filial debt, this took up a great deal of time. In fact, sometimes he felt he had just finished when he had to start all over again. When his wife Soo Ling was alive this had been her job. Now it had fallen to him.

Of course, Wee Kiat reflected, as he made his way down Canal Road towards the bridge over the Singapore River, with only two children apiece, his sons wouldn't do as well as he was doing and the thought brought him a feeling more akin to smugness than any real regret. But he was honest enough to admit, at least to himself, that his own enviable circumstance was less his doing than a question of a government holding itself back from unnecessary interference. And then things changed. The policy restricting family size – ONE MORE TO FEED, LESS FOR THE REST – that had been brought in just as his first child reached adulthood had forced each of his sons and daughters to limit the number of their own children to two. From the start, it had been clear to Wee Kiat that this business of restriction was rather short-sighted considering it would amount to a reduced allowance for his children in their old age and thus more government dependence. So the real fault lay solely with the government, as usual, for its controlling measures, for its over-planning and judiciousness, for holding up this island as a world model at the expense of its own citizens. Happening all over, or so the newspapers said, but happening all over was not the same as happening at home. At the footbridge he slowed and a few steps later he stopped as he sometimes did to watch the river traffic.

At precisely that moment, a tourist hung about with the latest camera gear rounded a corner to see the old man leaning on the iron railing. He had woken up that morning with just this sort of wish in mind. Aha! What a shot that would make! He would snap the old man outlined against the river, coolie hat shading part of his wrinkled face, his ochre skin and white goatee beard a perfect contrast with the dark grey tunic he wore buttoned to the neck. What a dignified old bloke. And what a perfect shot against the background of the tall thin buildings bleached by the angle of the sun and leaning towards his lens like stacks of sugar cubes. And perhaps that red sampan with the big eyes painted on its stern to the left of the foreground. He would worry about the framing of the shot, the finer details, later. Main thing was to fix this one for all time. Another face to add to his collection; he'd really had to stalk his subjects this trip. He took three rapid photographs, fumbled in his bag for the zoom, swapped the lens, and again positioned the old Leica that Doris was always on at him to swap for one of those modern point-and-clicks with their instant snaps.

What was it that caused Wee Kiat to look up a scant moment before the shutter snapped? In all the commotion of that morning – the scattered crowd that threaded through a snarl of traffic both sides of the river, the merry-go-round of river boats with their stuttering engines, the lines of schoolchildren in their dark blue and white – how was it he spotted a somewhat overweight, red-faced, rather ordinary man half-crouching at the far corner of the street he'd just come up? Could it be that the *areca* had heightened his senses, had allowed him to pick up an alien field of energy endeavouring to enter his own?

It wasn't that this hadn't happened to him before, this blatant stealing of his image, because it had. Many times. And it had always irritated him more than a little. But it was only today that he realised it was likely to keep happening, that he was a part of old Singapore and despite the government's persistent and systematic replacement of new for old, old was what the tourists came in their jumbo loads to see. He turned away, his jaws working to gather juice, so even as he left the bridge he decided that although he disliked the old habit of spitting, he despised both his own government and this particular tourist more, and that the only way he could immediately relieve his anger was to direct a jet of betel-red spittle neatly over the railings into the oily river.

Sidney stood up, dropped the camera with its long black zoom so it thumped against his chest. Disgusting old man. Hard to believe he'd thought him dignified a moment before. He'd got three, but he could have got more; the close-up, he feared, would be a dismal blur. Nothing for it but to follow the fellow.

Wee Kiat shuffled along, regretting the loss of the betel quid, chewing instead on his annoyance. He might have overcome his irritation sooner if he hadn't turned down towards the quay only to see that the tourist was still following him. But Wee Kiat wasn't young and there was an advantage in this fact. As a youth, his anger would have built up, incident by incident, indelibly imbued with a scent and taste as strong as if it had been enclosed in a smoker. As it was he could afford to slip into his usual tea shop, to sit and breathe in the herby scent of the light gold liquid. As the tourist puffed past down the street, he smiled.

Unlike some of his friends who were more erratic in their collecting, Wee Kiat liked to think he went about his task in an orderly fashion, visiting his children chronologically from eldest to youngest. And so, since today was the first day of the month, his first stop was to call on his eldest son, the young Mr Lim, who was a bank manager. Those two words 'bank' and 'manager' in connection with this eldest child never failed to give him the sensation of his chest being one size too small for his heart and if there were a tendency to lose height with his advancing age, this was reversed at the precise moment he inclined his head in reply to the respectful bow from the doorman.

He was led to a tub chair outside the manager's suite of rooms. The leather of the chair gave an expensive squeak and he let his eyelids droop with the extravagance of the sound as he settled down to wait. Even if it took all day to see his eldest son, seated in such luxury he wouldn't mind. The order of the bank pleased him: the row of tellers in their plate-glass cages, the long lines of people waiting with their shoulders slumped and patient, the way they turned away with their faces alight with happiness and gratitude at receiving their own money back, the many fans all circling in the same direction at the same speed, the refrigerated air … he was sitting with his eyes half-shut listing these advantages to himself when the soft hiss of the circling door issued in the tourist.

Wee Kiat sat upright, his gaze as intent on the tourist as the tourist's had earlier been on him. Surely this man could not still be following him? He was tired of having his day intruded upon. It was unlikely, but then the only other explanation was that this was some coincidence and Wee Kiat was as wary of the oddities of coincidence as he was of having his image appropriated.

But Sidney's awareness was not of the same calibre as Wee Kiat's. He was fond of boasting what a focused man he was, not realising that focus has a downside in that it has something of an alliance with tunnel vision, and that the obstinacy of his focus was such that he regularly missed what was not directly in his path. Today he was in the bank for one purpose: to cash a draft. Looking on, Wee Kiat could see that the beautiful surroundings of the bank meant nothing to him, that he had simply joined the end of the shortest queue and started fishing around in the big puffy shoulder bag he carried, a receptacle that was surely more suited to a woman than a man.

Wee Kiat's eyes were still narrowed, but no longer with the drowsiness of indulgence, instead with the first stirrings of a plan. After all, he told himself, it takes but a grain of rice to tip the scales and he'd had enough. He noted that even in this shortest queue the tourist was fourth in line. Each visit, one of his habits was to time the tellers by the big round clock that hung on the wall opposite and in all the time he had been coming here, not one of them had serviced a client in under two minutes; in fact, the average was somewhere between three and four, which his son boasted was the most efficient service in Singapore, if not the entire world. So, at best, it would take six minutes for the tourist to reach the front of the queue; if Wee Kiat was lucky it could take as long as ten or twelve.

Minutes later, Wee Kiat was in the deep-carpeted outer expanse of his son's office. The young Mr Lim was just finishing up with a client and normally his father enjoyed this scene too, this glimpse into his son's day, how tall and handsome he was as he shook the hand of one of his eminent clients and how even the gold rims of his smart eyeglasses glinted with confidence and prosperity. But today he was impatient with the ritual, with the seconds that slipped past in the greetings and in the small ceremony of ordering tea.

The young Mr Lim not only respected his father, but he was also very fond of him. He had treated his mother well so she had led a long and uncomplaining life and he had brought up his children in such a way that respecting the traditional and yet moving with the modern presented them with no difficulty and offered every advantage. Today, however, the young Mr Lim could see his father was agitated and that he wasn't concentrating properly on the particulars of his eldest grandchild's latest school report. In fact he wasn't a bit surprised when, after wincing at the too-hot tea, Wee Kiat jumped up and whispered something in his ear.

What he heard stirred his own anger. How dare a visitor to his country treat the old man with so little respect, treat his father as if he were little more than an animal caged in a zoo. Like his father he was superstitious about having his photograph taken. He had acquiesced to it uneasily for the sake of his banking career – but to take such a liberty without the courtesy of asking? And then to further harass his father by trailing him? Enough was enough. He picked up his telephone.

Ten minutes later Wee Kiat left and as he passed through the enormous banking hall he allowed himself a casual glance towards the tellers. What he saw made the skin around his eyes tighten, his lips move with mischief.

The tourist was having trouble. He kept jabbing at a piece of paper and the teller kept shaking his head. Wee Kiat sidled closer, so close in fact that as the tourist looked from one side to the other in his agitation, he did in fact stare right into Wee Kiat's face, although it wasn't until later he would remember that.

'But this is ridiculous,' Sidney was saying. 'I've never had any trouble before. Just wait until I get back home …' Yes, the teller agreed, but in this particular circumstance … Wee Kiat was passing out of earshot by this time, but he heard the tourist's demand to speak to the manager and he couldn't help a small chuckle, rubbing his hands briskly together as he went to step into the circle of the revolving doors.

A short while later, Sidney, too, emerged from the bank. He was on his way to meet his wife and had he been in less of a hurry he may have noticed the old man resting in a patch of shade. But as it was, he walked with his head down, his fists clenched and he would have passed by Doris as well had she not hailed him.

'Sidney, here, over here. What a ridiculous place to arrange to meet. If I'd known you were going to be this late, we could have met in a nice cool café somewhere …'

'I think we'd better get back to the hotel,' her husband said. 'I've just had the dickens of an argument with the bank … but first I want to find somewhere to get these films developed. Bound to be fewer places these days and they may take twenty-fours to process …'

At a discreet distance, Wee Kiat followed. He noted the photo shop, but it wasn't until he watched them disappear up the circular driveway between the curly-iron gates that led to their hotel, that he once again rubbed his hands. Fate was indeed on his side, proof he was in the right. He was enjoying himself more than he had at any time since Soo Ling had joined her ancestors. The allowance collecting might take a little longer this month, but it would be worth it. He pulled gently at his beard.

After a good lunch and long siesta, Sidney and Doris emerged from their suite at what they were fond of calling 'the civilised hour of five o'clock'. This was the time of day they enjoyed best. At this hour Doris was usually heard to say to Sidney, 'Well, I don't think anyone could say we're not putting our time here to good use' – the criterion of good use being the number of ticks against a list of things to see or buy, topped by this moment of wishing each other 'chin-chin' with big smiles on their faces as they clinked glasses. If she felt, as she did today, that this was the only time of day when her husband actually looked at her, such a thought was always quickly smothered.

But although they felt more rested than they had earlier, there was a mutual sense that the day hadn't gone quite as well as it could, the slightly uncomfortable feeling, not of failure exactly, but a type of flatness exacerbated by the fact that this was the last day of the holiday.

But as they lounged in the cushioned rattan chairs amid the pungency of sun-warmed honeysuckle, they found their dissatisfaction dissolving. Doris sipped at a Singapore Sling, Sidney a Tiger Lager, thinking that while there was nothing quite like a VB, there was something about the smoking coldness of the beers here, the chill and condensation on the glasses, the salted peanuts still in their papery wrappers. The large overhead fans pushed the heavy air pleasingly around the room and Doris was about to discuss plans for dinner when a waiter appeared to tell Sidney he was wanted at the hotel reception.

'Perhaps it's something to do with checking out, dear. I shouldn't rush if I were you. Finish your drink first.'

'Oh yes, of course, sir. I realise that, sir,' said the clerk when finally he fronted up at the reception desk. 'But we have a rule here that all accounts must be paid weekly unless you have a prior arrangement with the management. We tried to catch you this morning, sir, but you had already left for the day …'

'Well, it seems ridiculous to me,' Sidney expostulated for the second time that day. 'Do you mean I have to go all the way upstairs, get the cheques out of the safe and pay you for the week, and do the same thing tomorrow morning … all that just for one extra day?'

'If it would save you time, sir, you could pay the full eight days now and then you would have no problems checking out tomorrow. Or perhaps your credit card …'

'I don't use my cards in foreign countries and I want to use my traveller's cheques which is precisely the reason I bought them in the first place. I can't for the life of me see why …'

'I'm sorry, sir, this is the rule, long-time hotel policy, you see. Says so on the desk here, too …' And, sure enough, on the counter in front of him in large red capitals was a notice kindly requesting hotel guests to settle their accounts weekly.

Sidney gave in on that point, but on studying the bill he noticed he'd been overcharged for the room. He ran his fingernail under the figure. The clerk studied the account.

'Sir, but this is because you changed from a double room to a suite. That is correct? After the first night?'

'Yes, but had I known it was going to cost this …' he breathed deeply, 'that it was going to cost this much extra I would never have changed. Look here: this isn't what I was quoted.'

He was starting to feel a little off-colour. Taking a deep breath, he was about to ask to see the manager when Doris appeared at his side. He spun round to face her.

'Now, see what's happened,' he hissed. 'Just because you wanted more space and insisted on the suite, look what it's going to cost. A bloody arm and everything else. It's just as well we're leaving tomorrow, just as well, because we certainly won't have any money left. For anything. Perhaps not even the photos.' He glared at her. Quite apart from the last few, he had some impressive photographs in those rolls of film.

Doris sighed. It was not often Sidney got like this. It was the bank business that had upset him. She knew how important it was to him to get his precious pictures developed in the country of origin in case the airport x-ray machines wiped the film. He refused to go digital and it was becoming increasingly difficult to get them processed at home. She hoped he wasn't going to spoil the holiday.

The manager, a tall and elegant Singaporean, was polite but adamant. There must have been some misunderstanding because here it was, sir, written down in the brochure, that a suite cost so much, and that was that. He was sorry, very sorry.

On his way upstairs Sidney stopped on the landing to look into the courtyard below. This big square of green at the centre of the building, the borders lush with fragrant plantings, was one of the reasons he had stayed here more than once.

Catching his breath, he lingered long enough for his gaze to alight on what he thought was yet another opportunity to capture what he called a character-face in a different setting, *if* he'd been in the mood for photography, which he wasn't. He was about to head for the next short set of stairs, when he stopped to look back. Something in the way the chap held himself, his slim figure proud and straight despite his obvious age reminded him of somebody … reminded him of the Chinese bloke he'd photographed earlier. Was it chance that the old man looked up just then? That it was then that he raised his creased face and their gazes locked?

Sidney turned away abruptly. Suddenly he was glad he was going home the following day. Then in the upsetting period of paying money he was sure he didn't owe, he forgot all about him.

To make up for his bad humour, he suggested to Doris that as it was their last night, they might have a meal in Albert Street. They had done this on previous visits and he was hoping to salvage the evening. Silence on the part of his wife was a danger signal. So they took the Mass Transit to within cooee of Albert Street, placed their order for prawns and cashew nuts, barbecued spare ribs and fried rice, sat down to wait at one of the street tables.

'Last night, cheers.' Sidney smiled and raised his glass. But he'd barely brought the drink to his lips when his eyes bulged and he slapped down his glass. 'Well, bugger me.'

'What's the matter? Sidney? Whatever is the matter?' His wife's voice was higher than usual as he shook his head, rose half out of his chair. 'What's got into you this time?'

He was leaning on the table, breathing hard and staring at an elderly man sitting two tables away.

'Well? Do you see him?' Sidney almost spat. 'He's been following me about all day. Everywhere I go he's there.'

Her face brightened. Was that all? For a horrid moment she had thought the old chap was a drug peddler or something awful like that.

'Oh, Sidney, come on. There must be dozens of old fellows like that in Singapore. Look there's another. At the next table. There. Whatever are you on about?'

'Not like that one. Not like him. Believe me.' He put his hand on her arm. 'Come on, Doris, I've had enough of this. We're going.'

'Going?' His wife looked at him. 'I'm not going anywhere. I'm having the dinner I ordered right here at this table.'

At the pitch and sharpness of her tone, one or two of the surrounding diners stopped in their chewing and nattering to turn in their direction. One was indeed Wee Kiat who, all in all, had had a good day. Despite the time he had spent laying traps for the tourist, he'd seen two sons already. But this was unexpected. He started when he recognised Sidney. What a shame he hadn't known he was coming here tonight. This was one opportunity he'd have to pass on. He turned back to his meal, delicately squeezed his chopsticks to lift a tasty grain of rice. Tomorrow's little arrangement should fix the tourist for good.

Sidney had recovered a little by next morning. He could see now that he may have been rather foolish, that it was possible he had overreacted on more than one occasion the day before. To say he was sheepish would be overstating the degree of his remorse, but when Doris reassured him she had enough cash in her purse to pay for both photos and airport taxes, and suggested he go now, well in time to pick up the pictures, he stepped out of the room with just a hint of jauntiness. She was almost as proud of her husband's photos as he was himself. All of old people, they were. Oldies were the only photos worth taking, he always maintained, and when they had friends around he'd take them on a tour of what he called Sid's Gallery, pointing out the way the cheeks of the fair-skinned crumbled like tissue paper while those with more pigment in their skin creased like hide. He had some good photographs there. Everyone said so.

Except he shouldn't have taken the pictures of the people after the bus bingle, their eyes looking as though they didn't belong in the sockets. It made her uneasy; exactly why, she couldn't say, but perhaps it had something to do with the fact that they were trapped and exposed at a moment that was particularly personal. It was like photographing an animal in the wild giving birth, she'd said to him. You and your imagination, he'd retorted. You're talking about two entirely separate things. But she wasn't. She knew she wasn't. She just knew in her heart that there were some parts of people's lives that shouldn't be invaded.

She was nearly through with the packing, just one more case. This was the point at which she wondered whether she really needed the shoes with the seven-dwarf buckles, whether they were really as trendy as the salesperson had insisted. In the shop they had looked quite different. She hoped the luggage wouldn't be overweight.

So absorbed was she in what she was doing that a sudden furious hammering at the door caused her to clutch at the neckline of her blouse before she thought to take a breath. She looked at her watch. Sidney shouldn't be back yet.

'Is that you?' she called out.

'Of course it's me,' shouted Sidney, leaning so hard on the door that he all but fell inside when she opened it. He was shaking, almost sobbing.

She sat him on the bed, turned on the kettle. It was almost forty years since her father had taken her aside, quite some time before the wedding, certainly with room enough for her to change her mind. 'I think the guy you've chosen will make a steady-enough husband,' he'd said in his careful way, 'that is, until things don't go his way … That's when you might have to step in, dear, step in and take over the reins. See what I'm saying?' She saw, all right, but from what she also saw, most marriages were like that anyway so she didn't let it deter her from her plans. What her father's alert did do, however, was to make her determined to divert as many threats as she could from Sidney's path, to deflect anything that presented a challenge, to manage his life. Most times she was successful.

Now all she could think was to get him quietened down and back home.

They were starting to lose altitude on the run-in to Perth airport before Sidney showed any life at all. Looking straight ahead, without taking his gaze from the plane's jerky passage across the flight screen, he reached into his handbag to withdraw three Kodak envelopes which he handed sideways to his wife.

The beginning of a return to normality. Doris flicked open the flap and withdrew the first wad of photos, primed her smile.

She gazed, unbelieving at first. But, yes, it was so. Something had gone amiss. Each piece of glossy photo card was a blank. Completely unmarked. It was unlike Sidney, but he couldn't have wound on the film properly. He would insist on his damned old-fashioned contraction when one of the new digitals would be so much lighter. Easier to use, lighter to pack. And no stuff-ups like this. No wonder he was so upset. She reached across to squeeze his elbow, but he continued to stare straight ahead.

She opened the second envelope more slowly, hesitating because something in her suggested that this batch, too, might be blank. She fanned out their snowy whiteness and then her hands collapsed in her lap. After some minutes, silently she replaced the photos, was about to hand them back to him when, still not taking his gaze from the screen, he nudged her. His jaw moved.

'The other one. That last one.' he said out of the corner of his mouth.

Reluctantly she opened the third envelope, thinking at first that this was yet another pack of blanks, but, no, there was something on the final card. She studied it carefully, not because she was interested, but because she was stalling for time, for a clue as to what might have gone wrong and how it could have been prevented.

Besides, even this sole photo wasn't up to his usual standard. The face he had obviously been trying to snap was a blur – something like the desperate flutter of a bird's wing – and the only thing clearly discernible, the only thing with any definition at all really, was a hot-red sampan resting on water so smooth it could have been cooking oil.

The boat had a face painted on the stern and because there was nothing else to occupy her attention in those bumpy moments before landing, she looked at it more carefully than she otherwise would. The face up close was quite frightening. More, much more, than the down-pointing mouth, it was the long and wavy eyebrows over eyes with irises big, black and slanting to one side of their bright whites, that gave the boat its fearsome appearance. A hellish look, actually.

Her next thought was why paint such an unpleasant message on the rear end of your home? And now it collided with a memory. She recalled an instant of anger after a burglary, a sense that it had been as much herself as her home invaded, and her determination, soon forgotten, that what their back door needed was a picture of a large ferocious dog.

Sidney was out of his seat and into the aisle before the plane had come to a stop and by the time she'd collected her things, he was several people ahead in the queue.

What was he doing leaving his camera behind? Clucking to herself, she wrenched it from where he had stuffed it hard down into the seat pocket, hung it around her own neck and moved out into the crush.

MY MOTHER WAS A RUSSIAN SPY

Scrawled on a square of cardboard tacked to a fence pole, the sign reads: *4 Sale. House, furniture, workshop, tools. Everything 2 go.* With the sign sagged or slipped, the arrow points to the sky. But with nothing more pressing to do, she swings onto the rutted track alongside the barbed-wire fence.

But it isn't the house she sees first as the eucalypts thin and she draws into a clearing: instead, it's a rather tough-looking yellowish dog standing alongside a man bending down to pull at the straps of an oversize rucksack. Until he stands up – and then there's both of them glaring at her, fierce as each other. As she rolls down the window of the old Ford, the sound of the forest crowds into the car.

'The sign,' she says, by way of a reason for intruding into his day.

'More activity up there,' he cocks his head at the noisy canopy, 'than there is down here. Everything still for sale, 'cept the dog,' he says. 'And me.' From his words, she thinks he might be trying for a bit of fun, but his voice has a bitterness to it that she can taste at the back of her own throat.

It certainly isn't much of a house. It might have been once – before the nails rusted out, the weatherboards sprung and the white ants got at the stumps – but now it lists like a ship on a sandy beach.

'Well, good luck,' she says, her own words sounding hard. She slips the car into gear. But perhaps it's some time since anyone wished this man luck and she's pleased to see him smile, his mouth slipped sideways like the house behind him. 'Are you selling up and leaving, then?'

He shrugs. 'Me ole Mum's crook. Goin' to look in on her.' He bends to pick up a rifle, rams it into the side of the backpack.

'I could give you a lift.'

'Across to Launceston?'

'You're not going to walk?' As she stares doubtfully at the old dog, the gun and the size of the pack, he speaks quickly to stop her thinking.

'Nah. Why would I walk when I got me 'copter parked out back.' Then he nods at the car. 'Besides you look like you've got your own house packed fairly tight in there. No room at that inn.' When he grins, he looks nice.

'So what are you going to do with all that?' She jerks her chin at the house.

'Can't pack it up and take it with me, can I?'

'You're just going to leave it empty?' Her voice rises and out of the corner of her eye she sees the dog move restlessly.

'Give the rats a home at least.'

'Are you coming back?'

She sees his gaze slide to his dog and then off into some place she can't see and she looks away herself. She knows from her own thinking that there are some things you can't think, even to yourself, let alone say. So she pretends to be very interested in the house, although to tell the truth there's not much to see after the first glance.

'Dunno. See what gives, I guess. Plans can do the dirty on a man.'

'Do you own it – the property?'

'Course I bloody own it. You think I stole it or summin? But there's nothing of real value. Only thing valuable is me mate here.' He cuffs the dog's ears, so the animal sticks its nose into his hand. 'And you? While we're on the twenty questions, why are you on the run? Not house-hunting surely?'

'Nothing to run from.' The forest suddenly silent as if the birds themselves are listening.

'Running to, running from, same diff.' He squints at the sky. 'Look, lady. Not sure just why you're out Sunday driving or what your own plans are. But we got to be getting on.' He reaches for his pack and just as suddenly stands up again. 'Tell you what though. Thought's just hit me. You look like you could do with a bit of a spell yourself. Why don't you take a look around the place and if it suits, hang out here for a spell? Key's on top of the old water heater under the mug by the back door.'

'Oh yeah? And my mother was a Russian spy.' She glowers.

'And there I was thinkin' we didn't have too much in common. I'd ask you in for a cuppa and some discussion around our respective Mums and their spying days, but I got no apple pie and I've gone and packed up me best china. Real pretty tea set, it is too. Yellow, with pink flowers round the edge. You'd have liked it.'

'Are you being funny with me?'

'In a manner of speakin', yes, I am. But what's with the upset? Just sayin' that if you've a mind to rest up, you could do me a bit of a turn at the same time.'

'Me?'

'Well, ain't it us b'n talkin?'

'I wasn't expecting. I can't pay you.'

'Wasn't talking money, was I? And I don't like the term 'favour' because that sets expectations popping like the pox. More like a house-sit. Grand home that it is. With all mod cons – apart from the dunny out back which is still one o' them bucket deals. Something of a store down the road where you can get the necessaries. Cans of juice too for that overstuffed jalopy you got there.'

She doesn't like his term for the car in which she's spent more nights than she cares to remember, but nevertheless she switches off the engine, opens the door.

'I could fix it up. Maybe.' She can see he's about to retort when his glance lands on her hands. You can tell a lot from a person's hands.

He shrugs on the pack. 'Whatever. Plenty tools in the shed. Just put the key back when you quit the joint.' She's still standing with her hand on the car door when he swings away. 'Come on fella, we're outa here or we won't be making a start till night.'

It's just then that a kookaburra starts its long laugh. He stops to look back over his shoulder, calls out over the warble. 'There's thems that say that bird is jeering. But how about it might just be cheering?' He raises his hand in a half-salute. 'Maybe we'll get to have that cuppa one day.' That grin again that mocks himself. 'Maybe we will and maybe we won't. So long kid.'

And that should have been the end of the story, watching the guy and his dog disappearing around the first bend. Any sensible girl would have got back in the car and left it at that, but she starts thinking how it would be polite to give him a little time to get going rather than passing him on the narrow track, which leads to a second thought and then another. He has left her with so much of the *maybe this and maybe that,* which in itself is a type of possibility, and she knows a person shouldn't turn away from possibilities. Besides, can she really afford to turn down an offer of a free bed, even if it is just for one night?

So she goes around the back of the place to find that the key is just where it should be and that the door opens easily enough. But then it sticks and as she pushes on it she can see the way it has eaten into the green lino through having been opened so often. She steps back to see that it is just that the top hinge has lost a couple of screws and that it can be fixed with no trouble at all. The place is rundown, no doubt about that, but clean enough – the rats he spoke of would have no joy here. The bed has been stripped, but she finds some unironed sheets in a drawer in the kitchen.

Out back, just as he said, the shed is stacked high with tools left higgledy-piggledy on the bench and over the floor. She clasps her hands. A terrible mess on the one hand, a carpenter's dream on the other.

Not knowing just when the store might close, she decides to go out earlier rather than later for food and provisions, but it's not until she's bumping along the track towards the highway that she remembers the sign. It could mean people driving up at odd times just as she did herself, but since he'd given her no selling instructions, he may well have decided to take it down. But then again, presumably he still has a need to sell? And, sure enough, as she approaches, she sees that there it hangs.

But now it's been turned back to front with something scratched into the paint. When she gets out to look more closely, it is then she reads:

SOLD: To the pretty daughter of the Russian spy ☺

MEMOIR

‘TO LEAVE OR NOT TO LEAVE?
IT’S NOT SO SIMPLE.’

I have a South African friend who refuses to leave the country of his birth. He inherited a farm in the north-east of the Transvaal that had been in his family for generations and over the years he and his South Australian wife have built up an orchard of some repute. Despite a recent attack on his life, he is determined to continue with his life in South Africa.

'There are the people who say we're lucky to be alive,' he said in a recent email. 'That after what we've been through, we should not tempt fate, and just walk away. But it's not so simple.

'Yes, it's true, they may kill me. But this is my life: this country, our farm and livestock, those friends we still have here. If we walk away, if we return to my wife's city of Adelaide, what would I do for the last twenty years of my life? Sit on the verandah and watch the sun go down over the hills? At sixty-five years of age, I'm too old to start again from scratch, too young to waste the time left to me pretending I'm having a great time "travelling". I love my home and my work. To leave or not to leave? It's not so simple.'

My first thoughts on receiving this were that it could be argued there were other choices, that there are always other choices; but when I came to think about it, I wondered just how realistic, how workable, these really were.

Homesickness – the illness that can follow from leaving the land of your birth, a home you love or a way of life you identify with and which has become integral to your own sense of identity – is still one of the most unexplored and unrecognised forms of disease in an era when we're paranoid about things on the micro-scale of the risks of butter versus margarine.

Please listen while I tell you the story of my mother, an Englishwoman, who loved every moment of the sixteen years she spent in Africa. While today she would be labelled orientalist, this was well before the writings of Chinua Achebe and Edward Said and the world was a very different place. The story of my mother, my father and the African connection begins in a London torn apart by the blitz.

London

Mum loved the war. She was by then in her mid-twenties, a person who romanticised danger and relished excitement – just as she was later to romanticise and relish Africa – and she was at her best when faced with situations that would make many of us tremble. There was, for instance, the day a doodle-bug narrowly missed Australia House in London where she worked as head telephonist.

Later she said, 'We – the telephone exchange – were on the top floor with a ceiling made of glass that split open and shattered with the force of the blast. There were shouts, someone screaming. The room filled with flying shards, splinters. In ten seconds it went from quiet to complete chaos. I pushed my young assistant Jeannie under the desk and turned to the switchboard. I've never seen anything like it, you know, not before or since. A fairyland of flashing lights. A fairyland on the one hand and something quite the opposite on the other.'

Quietly, calmly, with one hand shielding her head from the falling glass, she fielded the frenzied ferocity of those calls, soothing, informing, reassuring friends and family that both Australia House and nearby Bush House had missed a direct hit. I've seen my mother work one of those switches, her long fingers with the smoothly manicured red nails blurring with speed as her hands flick from one cord to another, her voice never losing its instinctive kindness, its self-assuredness. That was one side of my mother.

But there was another, and she was just as focused on her subtle play for Kenneth Coton, a young Australian lieutenant at Bush House, who first got her attention by placing files on her desk marked ACTION in large red capitals. He was an attractive man of middle height some eleven years older than she, and although at first she judged him just a little too arrogant and sure of himself, ultimately, of course, this was just the sort of challenge my mother couldn't resist. She worked hard at winning his total love until by the end of the war she had dispatched the competition and was planning her final strategy.

There is no doubt Dad was attracted to her from the first, but he had been caught once and he was wary. Besides, he had other plans. The end of the war saw him in consultation with a business consortium that planned to set up a cassava plantation in what was then Southern Rhodesia. However, before he left, he asked my mother if she would be prepared to join him in Africa. As far as I know, at this point the M-word hadn't been discussed. And this was back in 1946, remember, when well-brought up young girls were cautious. Ostensibly, at least.

'You'll have to talk to Ruby,' was my mother's answer.

My mother was June Daynes, the seventh child in a family of eight with a mother confined to a wheelchair while the two eldest girls acted as surrogate matriarchs to their younger siblings. Perhaps because of the responsibility they had to bear, both Zena and Ruby were rather stern no-nonsense women, but practical, too, in that they made sure all the children – girls as well as boys – were educated or tutored in one trade or another. My mother, for instance, trained as a tailor which, as it turned out, served her well. But when my father approached Ruby, out of a sense of courtesy rather than permission-seeking, he was advised in no uncertain terms *not* to encourage June to join him.

'My sister is a rambling rose, Ken. And quite, *quite* wild. If it's my opinion you want, you would be absolutely crazy to take her on, or to take her out to the colonies, particularly a place like *Africa*. She'll be back in no time,' said Ruby. But if Aunt Ruby thought her insistence would be a deterrent, she was quite wrong. She was wrong, too, in thinking that Africa would not be right for my mother. From the moment she arrived, it clad her like a veil of silk, clinging, caressing and colouring her emotions – and the rest of life – from that day on.

My father went out first to set up the cassava venture, which failed quite quickly, partly because he was ahead of his time, partly because he was swindled by his partners. Coming out of this experience with his core unfazed, he bought a small mixed farm instead, quite ignoring the fact that his skills and experience in Melbourne – initially in his father's antique business and then in journalism, followed by the war years in both the British and Australian armies in London – weren't a natural fit for farming anywhere, let alone Africa.

My parents were very different, but – without being too simplistic about this – I believe they both had the same approach to risk with the result they evaluated it more for the opportunity it contained than the threat it posed. They were both glass-half-full people – at least in the early days.

Southern Rhodesia

It would not have been many months after he left that my mother, blithely free of the Daynes' family, travelled out to join him, sailing with his mother Eileen in a converted warship where they slept in hammocks and ate mess-style below decks from long wooden tables.

What was Southern Rhodesia like in those days? What sort of expatriate life was my mother heading towards? What was this lure from which she was never to break free?

Piecing it together more from what wasn't said as was, I would guess the farmhouse they lived in at first was a dwelling that was little more than a brick and iron shelter that from time to time my mother would refer to as the *banda*. The property was more of a subsistence farm than anything else – goats, chickens and a few cows for milk and butter alongside a small acreage of tobacco, mixed crops and vegetables. My father's later love of carpentry manifested in these early days in his fashioning of the wooden forms that he and his African workers filled with mud and baked in the sun to form building bricks for extensions to the main living area of the *banda* and outhouses.

And the life they led? The life my mother couldn't let go?

It started with a ride across the dry grasses of the savanna as the sun rose in the early mornings. They arrived home to hand the reins of their horses to the *syce*. After breakfast, Dad would go off to his farm concerns and Mum would make curtains and tablecloths for the home, sew the crisp white uniforms for the house staff, design and cut out her next dress and plan the sundowner parties she came to love.

'In Rhodesia, at one point, I had eight servants,' she told me once. 'The Africans would come and knock at the door of the *banda* – young and old they were, men and women with barely a full garment between them. We had no language between us in the early days, but we communicated in something other than words: we understood each other. They wanted jobs and they could see I had little to offer in terms of either work or pay in that tiny place. But they'd heard about the smartness of the uniforms I made and something, it appeared, about us. And they were eager to learn. So they came: some made cooks, some made gardeners and some helped your father on the farm. I taught them what I could – although, actually, I think I learned more than I taught. When they were ready, they left. It was always that an aunt had died or a cousin had fallen sick, but by then I had enough of their language – both silent and spoken – to know that it was their time to move on.'

Often she would go riding by herself and I can see her reining in her horse – stopping from time to time with her head on one side, her brow furrowed with the will to miss nothing, to indulge herself in one of her greatest pleasures – listening to the murmur of the bush.

'It has a buzz and a beat, the African bush,' she said to me more than once. 'Not something you hear, so much as something you feel. Just here.' She put her hand over her heart. 'And in your blood. A sort of fizzing in your veins.' The nights she loved, too. 'The darkness has a texture to it,' she often said, 'like brushing up against the softest velvet.'

She had a small handgun, a Beretta, of which she was enormously proud. I don't know whether she ever used it, but this was bush, a mix of thicket, savanna grassland, thorn trees and tall, toppling rock *kopjes*. Lions, in particular, were common although it was probably the baboons that presented the most danger. Snakes, too, were plentiful – poisonous snakes – and for all her time in Africa, she carried a kit with scalpel, swab, a small bottle of permanganate and a tourniquet.

'If you get bitten, there'll be two marks,' she told me. 'Keep your head. Make a cut over the marks, suck hard, spit out the poison. Spit. Then tie a bandage tight just above it to stop the poison going to your heart. Then get help. Quick as you can.'

My mother had a pair of crocodile-skin shoes she had stained herself in a sort of purplish-mauve colour and they lived at the rear of the wardrobe. Perhaps it was the reptilian leather that struck the female snake as a compatible place to unload her eggs because when next my mother pulled out the shoes, a writhing mass of baby black mamba spilled out. That would have been enough for many women to head back to England: for my mother, it was a good story to tell at dinner parties.

They lived just out of Marandellas – now Marondera – going up to Salisbury (Harare) rarely, and I think it was this period of her life in Africa that took over my mother's imagination so completely that later, when she referred back to Africa, it was these first few years in that strange and beautiful country, that filled her heart and her mind. They lived the country itself, not just the sights or famous wonders of it, so when in later years my mother was asked what she thought of Victoria Falls, she would reply in a mix of surprise and confession that she hadn't actually visited the falls and that their lives were so full it was not something that crossed their minds.

It was her miscarriage after being dumped by a rogue wave while holidaying in Beira that prompted them to get married. The dress she made for her wedding was of a green silk crepe she had asked one of her sisters to send from England. The pattern she cut out of newspaper. She kept that dress her whole life and the only place I've seen that colour duplicated is in the impossibly green Gulf waters off the coast of Saudi Arabia.

Southern Rhodesia was a sociable place in those days when people would think nothing of driving sixty or seventy miles over rutted dirt roads to attend a party on a neighbouring property where they would overnight before travelling home the next morning. After dinner, while the men told inappropriate jokes or 'visited Africa' to urinate into the darkness, the women would retire to change into housecoats, returning to relax with the men over coffee and brandies before bed.

By the time my mother was expecting me, they'd made many friends, among them Peter Wynter, a German medical doctor who had emigrated to Southern Rhodesia at the end of the war and who, being German, was at that time still prohibited from practising. Completely disregarding this, my mother asked Peter to deliver me, her first baby, and their nineteen-year-old daughter Dagmar to be my godmother. Dagmar went on to make a name for herself in Hollywood as Dana Wynter and, somewhat ironically given her German background and the position her father had been in when he first came out to Rhodesia, she took the lead female role as an officer in the British Royal Navy in *Sink the Bismarck.*

Cape Town

It was 1950 and I was about 18 months of age when my parents left Southern Rhodesia for the Cape. Just why they left was never explained, possibly it was driven by the necessity of a job beyond the uncertainty of the little farm. In Cape Town, they rented a house high up the hillside in a spot called Gordon's Bay which looked out towards the lights of Table Mountain. My father found work as a sales representative which meant he was away all day, and compared with the social calibre of the life they had just left, this must have been a very different life for them both and a lonely period for my mother.

By this time we had acquired a dog, a Ridgeback/Mastiff called Flash who set the standard for all dogs I've owned since. He let me ride him, pull his ears, clean his teeth and brush him endlessly. All day, like the hound he was, he slept beside me, and I adored him. But at base he was Mum's dog, ferociously loyal and – unfortunately – a savage fighter.

One day a man purporting to be a hawker mounted the one hundred and fifty steep steps from the road. The front door was the stable type with the top half open to catch the breeze; my mother was alone with me, sewing as usual on her Sapphir treadle machine. Whatever his goods, she was not interested and she told him so. But, undeterred, he placed his hand on the lower half of the door before reaching over for the bolt on the inside. That was enough for Flash who, in one powerful movement, uncoiled from where he had been lying beside me to take off over the door. The man fell backwards, rolled down the steps and we were never bothered by pedlars from that time on.

Tororo via Nairobi

I'm guessing that South Africa didn't work out too well because before long we were on the move again – sailing from Cape Town up the coast to East Africa where my father had a job lined up at the veterinary laboratory – or vet lab as they called it – in Nairobi.

This time I think we only stayed put for six months before setting off again for Tororo in Uganda, not far from the Kenyan border. My father was now a 'buyer' for Tororo Cement, the huge cement works that was the town's (only) claim to fame. And it's only now I ask myself: what did 'buyer' actually mean? Was it that he sourced the raw materials for the plant? It was never clear and I'm not sure I ever questioned it.

All this travel cost money they didn't have, and this was when my mother's tailoring training came in very handy indeed. She had always made her own garments and now she took in sewing. I was nearly four and it is from this period that my memory kicks in. Me sitting playing beside her with Flash curled banana-shape around me as she turned out garment after garment, the thump and rhythm of the treadle following me in my dreams.

But things were changing, at home and overseas. Suddenly I had a little sister – Toni – so there was a degree of separation between my mother and me that had not been there before. It was 1952 and the newspapers were full of the coronation of Queen Elizabeth. Hanging on the wall behind the counter tops of the local *dookas*, the faded framed photographs of George VI were replaced with the bright face of the young queen in the lace gown with the royal-blue sash.

This, too, is where I start to see Africa with my own eyes. It's only in looking back from a distance of some years that I get a fragile glimpse of what my mother experienced, and to some extent that picture is coloured for me by what came later. Back then, I had no other frame of reference: Kenya, Uganda and Tanganyika were just countries where I happened to grow up. While shopping at the market for our daily food, for example, I wasn't comparing the frenzy around me – heaping piles of red, yellow and gold spices, stacks of massed vegetables and the *mabibi* in their vibrant multi-patterned *kikois* – with Pinner main street, Middlesex, on a windy day where the women wrapped themselves in thick felty coats and scarves. I didn't know, either, that there were places as grey as their skies when what I was used to was our afternoon thunderstorm at four o'clock, when the clouds would build until the thunder split and shook above our heads, the lightning flashed and the rain hissed down, only to return to cloudless minutes later. In Moshi, Tanganyika, I took for granted the view of Mt Kilimanjaro from the front door of our house, so close the snow looked soft enough to lick. Or driving back home after a holiday to the coast, I didn't share my mother's awe and astonishment when we found a herd of elephant – probably about fifty of them, their hides gold as the setting sun – taking a dust bath alongside our garden boundary. At the time, making more impact on me than the elephants was her tight intake of breath, her hand on my father's arm, the tone in which she spoke.

'Oh,' she breathed, 'just look at that.'

Because I had not known anything different, what was amazing or special about Africa for my mother was for me quite ordinary.

Except the abattoir. Occasionally, if she couldn't get the cut of meat she wanted from the fly-covered carcasses hanging on hooks to one side of the vegetable market, my mother would go direct to the abattoir, a type of corral some way out of the township with walled sides built too high for a four-year-old to see over. When I asked to be lifted up, she looked at me doubtfully.

'Are you sure?'

When I nodded, she lifted and held me – briefly – with my eyes above the wall. Some sights never leave you, but in this case it involved all my senses. My mother's long nails dug into my sides while I gripped the top of the barrier. Down below, the cattle were milling in a tight circle, their lowing a long, raucous wail, their heads raised high so their eyes shone white through the dust; there was the rancid odour of terror mixed with the sweet smell of blood, the blade of a knife flashing silver in the sunlight.

Safer, much safer, to remember the pinkish-purple of the permanganate of potash my mother used to sterilise the water to soak any vegetables we didn't grow ourselves. Or the safe – a flywire-encased set of shelving – around which the servants hung freshly washed dishcloths, both to cool the produce inside and to dry the cloths. Much later, we acquired a second-hand fridge, a temperamental piece of equipment that rumbled constantly and worked spasmodically on copious amounts of paraffin. All our drinking water was boiled. On long leave in England when I was five, I was shocked and upset when my aunt poured me a glass of water from the tap. I can still remember the hoots of laughter that greeted my uncertain question: 'But why isn't it boiled?'

Another regular East African event fell into my dread-list: the countless injections, vaccinations and boosters that were Africa. Usually a small medical team would visit to set up in one of the schools and my overriding memory is of a quadrangle of white-faced children. Smallpox was all right because it was only a scratch. Yellow fever was bad because of the regularity of the repeats; typhoid was worse because it made your arm ache. Then the polio vaccine was introduced. The other precautions didn't seem so bad at the time. The daily anti-malarial tablet Paludrine was useful as a bed-delaying tactic and memories linger of the DDT-filled flit gun and the mist that drifted down to settle damply over our faces every night of our childhood.

One day Flash was missing. I was so used to his disappearing to have one flank or another stitched after a fight that it was some time before I thought to ask my mother where he was. When eventually, to my surprise, she emerged from the linen cupboard at the end of the passage she knelt beside me. Her face was red and blotchy and, without asking, I knew. That dog had fought his last battle and I'd lost my best and most constant friend.

Eldoret, Mombasa, Moshi, Nairobi

But change was ever on the prowl. At age six, it was boarding school for me at Loreto Convent, Eldoret, just over the border in Kenya and it was from this phase of my own life I first experienced homesickness – the crippling despair that can thread and bind tight with the feeling of loss. It was only a term later that I rejoined the family, but to me it felt (both then and now) like half my life.

In the short time I had been away, my father had joined Pepsi – or Pepsi-Cola as it was then – as manager of the Mombasa branch. So I had left the house where my first real memories had been formed and three months later returned to another home in another country – which possibly set in place a habit which lingers still: the visiting of each room in a house to say goodbye whenever I've left a home in which I've been happy.

Mombasa was only ever meant to be for six months; instead of a straight-out rental, we were housesitting a pretty bungalow that was once again built on a hill, but this time with a resident cat we were to care for while the owners were on long leave.

My recollections of this seaside town are few, but vibrant: my parents bargaining for Persian carpets as the dhows docked at the quayside; the death of the cat following an operation on a cancerous growth; a brick thrown at my mother that missed and smashed the window behind her head one night; the intensity of shame I experienced on my first day at my new school, another Loreto, notable for its particularly attractive uniform of white, square-necked tunic and red girdle.

That first day, when my father turned to leave me just inside the gates, with memories of being left at boarding school still sharp in my mind, I slipped my fingers into the belt loops of his trousers and hung on tight. Children's fingers are strong, and terror made my hands lock tighter than a Staffie's jaw. It took two nuns to disentangle me and walk me to one of the wooden benches in the huge hall where morning assembly had already started. But the greatest indignity of all was wetting my pants. I sat there until the hall emptied, hunkered down, willing my smart new uniform to dry and hoping the nuns would leave me there until home-time. The rest of my time there is a blur. I learned nothing.

Six months later, Dad was transferred to the small town of Moshi nestling in the foothills of Mt Kilimanjaro in Tanganyika and, despite the series of rented homes over the next three years, it was here my mother really began to enjoy herself once again.

I remember Moshi, too, for Miss Innes, the headmistress of the primary school. Before she accepted me into her school, she had insisted on an interview with me that both parents also attend. During the meeting she gave me a pencil and paper and asked me to write down the words I knew. I was seven by then. I could write my name and remember digging deep for *fox* and *dog*, but when she asked me to write *Mummy* and *Daddy*, I failed totally. I remember her looking at me closely, that kind woman, and saying that I was just the sort of person she'd like to have in her class.

That was all it took. I started reading. I started writing. I learned there was no such word as *can't*. Less than a year later I wrote my first short story. It was titled "The King's Cabbages"; my mother kept it in her red folder with her important papers through all our many moves and so I have it still. Back in Moshi, when Miss Innes eventually married and became Mrs Boulé we took her a wedding present. But brilliant and committed teacher that she was, perhaps the best present I could have given her, and didn't, would have been the knowledge that at my next school – a convent again and this time in Nairobi – I would come top of class each term for the three years I was there.

By the time we moved to Nairobi, the Mau Mau was in its last phase. To show their appreciation of what Dad had achieved at the Mombasa and Moshi plants, the big guns of PepsiCo International in their plush offices back in the United States offered to build us a house. So, on an acre of land with an avenue of jacaranda trees down one side – originally planted by the nuns to link the convent with a monastery – we lived in the first home since the *banda* that wasn't a rental.

It was set on the side of a slight hill, so beyond the borders of the garden was a sweep of pale brown grassland that ran down into a slight valley and up the other side. For some reason, my mother had chosen a German Black Forest design for the house which called for a steeply pitched black-tile roof, a cedar-clad second storey and dormer windows.

She was photographed in front of that house for one of the country's leading home magazines. It's not her best photo, her eyes are tensed against the sun and she looks too prim for my mother. But there's something else about that photograph: it's hard to pin down, but it's not pride alone that speaks from that glossy front cover. A sense of completion perhaps, the roots of the rambler digging deep into the clinging clay. Just as she kept the first-ever story I wrote, I've kept that magazine cover.

Outside the downstairs' windows my mother planted sixty tea roses and I grew up knowing their idiosyncrasies and each of their names: Peace, Papa Meilland, Queen Elizabeth and the deep butter-yellow Buccaneer (the last secretly close to my heart because I was getting old enough to romanticise a pirate as a potential mate and life as a perpetual treasure hunt). Our bedrooms were on the second floor – mine decorated in blue, with blue-and-white gingham curtains, Toni's in pink – and we looked into the branches of the jacarandas that for two months of the year showed-off in a cloud of bluish-purple splendour. It was a lovely house that became a home.

This was another good chapter for my mother. After a married life of rented houses, she now had her own home. There's no denying there was a lot of 'white mischief' in East Africa as director Michael Radford's film of that name depicted. The conditions were ripe for it. The vast majority of expatriate white women in those days were wives who were privy to a plentiful supply of time and enough money, headily free from the shackles of 'the family back home' and either over-stimulated by their new environment or homesick and open to consolation. Parties and social gatherings were frequent, the police force wasn't interested in controlling the drinking habits of its citizens and my mother was able to indulge her flirtatious side.

'But,' she said to me one day as I sat reading in her sewing room. 'Let me make this clear. A kiss is just a kiss and doesn't have to go any further.' She went on to assure me she had been completely faithful to my father and intended to remain so. 'What's more,' she added, 'I tell your father everything.' I was too young to really understand what she was saying and too naïve for it to worry me. But not so young that her words didn't stick.

The sundowner parties that had been so much part of her life in Southern Rhodesia she made her particular speciality: the full range of drinks and mixes accompanied by platter after tasty platter of little toasty squares dabbed with caviar, overstuffed creamy vol-au-vents, wickedly salty Devils on Horseback, small pinwheels of salmon and cream cheese, little carved orange baskets filled with fresh cubes of fruit. Not for her, the pickled onion, pineapple and cheddar on a toothpick.

I would huddle in the shadows, just around the bend in the stairs, staring through the curls of wrought-iron at the elegance of the women in their cocktail dresses, the men in their white jackets, the pitches of laughter, the clink – and sometimes the shatter – of glass.

She played a lot of bridge and each week we went to the races, dressed to impress with the lovely clothes she made us, while she won and lost on her five-shilling bets.

When, a couple of years later, she applied for and was granted a Kenyan passport to replace her English one, you would think she'd gone to God.

Decisions

But in the politically charged environment of the day, it was inevitable that big adjustments lay just ahead. Harold Macmillan's 'wind of change' was starting to blow across the continent of Africa. When the 1960 speech he gave on a visit to South Africa was printed in the *East African Standard*, my mother sneered.

'It'll never happen. Not in my lifetime anyway.'

But Macmillan was right and my mother was wrong. Change with its freedom call had started in the northern half of the continent the decade before and now it was East Africa's turn to extract itself from the collapsing Empire, to obliterate the pink bits from the map. The time had come for *Uhuru*. Kenya was scheduled for Independence in 1964 and my mother knew time was limited.

She started making a list of pros and cons: the positives limited to the single word 'children'. But it was Adija – the *ayah* who had been with us through so many moves she was now less an *ayah* than a friend – who spoke first.

'But, *Memsahib*, what will happen to us now? Now everyone is leaving?'

'*Shauri ya Mungu*, Adija. It is the will of God. *Kweli.* They call it progress and one day you will be better off. Perhaps you will work for an African person? I will give you an excellent reference. Or maybe you will return to your *shamba*? I am so sorry – I too wish this weren't so. Believe me, I also … I so wish we could stay.' She glanced across at me and her voice was softer and troubled. 'It's because of the children, you see. *Watoto*, Adija, *sababu watoto*.'

Adija looked down at her feet and up towards the window. Finally, she gave a small shrug.

'*Sejui, Memsahib. Sejui.*' She sighed. But then something happened, and they were no longer employer and employee – black and white in their separate spaces – but two women who'd arrived at a place where language is superfluous. For a long minute they gazed at each other, their eyes uncertain, mouths working. It was Adija who looked away first. She breathed deeply. '*Labda*,' she conceded. '*Labda*.' Maybe. She bent forward to pick up something from the floor, a long slow sweep of a movement, and the lead in her pencil broke as my mother added another mark to the list on the right of the page.

To look back with post-Edward-Saidian hindsight distorts the reality of how things were in East Africa in the Fifties and early Sixties: that our relationship with our servants – particularly in comparison to the southern part of the continent – was in the main excellent and uncomplicated. It was only eight years afterwards when I was newly married and living in South Africa that I found how very different it was from East Africa in this respect. In Johannesburg, I had an uncomfortable relationship with home-help undercut as it was with an uneasy combination of subservience and aggression. Of course, the change in attitude could be ascribed to the time interim, but perhaps not. East African servants carried themselves with pride and dignity. This fragment from J. M. Coetzee's fictionalised memoir *Summertime* suggests that regardless of sharing the same landmass, the two parts of the continent are poles apart. Says the character Sophie in Coetzee's story: 'That was one of the surprising things I discovered about South Africa: how insular it was. I went back on a visit last year, and it was the same: little or no interest in the rest of Africa. Africa was a dark continent to the north, best left unexplored.' When you talk – or write or think – about Africa, it is dangerous and inaccurate to lump South and East together. For that matter, all African nations have significant cultural differences.

In common with many other white children, during much of my childhood in some ways I was closer to my *ayah* than my mother. All our family spoke, with varying degrees of fluency, the language of the country and by the time I was four I knew as many Swahili words as I did English. Being off-limits to us children, the servants' quarters were of course irresistible. In most of the houses we rented they were separate from the main house, usually two or three small rooms with an area to ablute and another to cook. In comparison with some of the *au pair*'s attic rooms I've seen in France or the *amah*'s mean little bed often part of the kitchen in the majority of Hong Kong flats, these were spacious. The Africans did most of their cooking – usually a big pot of stew, either vegetable or meat, that tempted from wherever we were in the garden – on a charcoal brazier or Primus stove. Another huge pot would contain *posho*, a dough made from maize flour, a piece of which they would roll into a steaming ball, press with a thumb to make a scoop and dip into the stew. Or sometimes the meal would be *mealies* – corn cobs – charred on the coals that would bring us sniffing at the air like hounds before we were chased away.

But the single positive for leaving Africa – the children – won the day and my father worked on Pepsi for a transfer to Australia which for him, of course, was home. A transfer, it appeared, was out of the question, but they would offer him a position once he was in the country. My friend Anne promised she'd write every day. Adija cried. My mother's best friend Aunty Mon was devastated. I was excited. My first time on a plane. We flew to Aden to board the ship.

Living in Africa with regular tours 'back home', we were familiar with voyages. But this was my mother's first experience of a one-class ship, the *Fairsea* – built as a migrant ship in 1949 – and she rapidly discovered that one-class meant tourist-class. It was also the era of the 'ten-pound passage' and it didn't help that a large proportion of passengers – Greek and Italian wives or widows perhaps – were draped from head to toe in black. It didn't help, either, that the couple with whom we shared the dinner table habitually ordered the menu in reverse. All small things in the context of life, but unbeknown to us, there was a sickness starting in my mother and she was ready to be appalled.

We docked at Fremantle, our first taste of our new country and of a day that went too quickly for me. But when we arrived back at the wharf ready to board for the last stage of our journey through the turbulent Bight, my mother stopped at the gangplank to stare out to sea, past the busy wharf and its cranes, across the winey darkness of the Indian

Ocean, back the way we'd come. Just then the sun came out and the surface of the sea shimmered with silver spangles. She turned to me, her eyes wild, gripped my shoulders.

'Never look back,' she said fiercely. 'Never, ever, look back.'

I knew, even then, she was talking to herself, not me.

Sydney

When the ship finally docked in Sydney, there was excitement in Dad to be back in the city of his birth, but the immigration officials looked askance at my mother's Kenyan passport, conferring among themselves before fumbling around for another stamp which they pressed evenly onto the inking pad, from there to the watermark at the centre of the page. The officer pushed the document back towards my mother. 'Next.'

My mother opened the passport, her hands not quite steady. 'Alien. Alien?' Again she looked down at the stamp and then up my father. 'I'm an *alien* here?'

The bad start was compounded by the meanness of the Sydney flat and by Toni and I catching chicken pox. A chilly, windy month of May in a strange town with two irritable, feverish, scratching children whom she threatened on the one hand and dabbed with pale pink calamine lotion on the other – both methods designed to stop the itching. But true to their word, Pepsi did offer Dad a job. As manager of the plant in Port Augusta.

Port Augusta

Things may well have changed, but I think it's fair to say that fifty years ago Port Augusta was one of Australia's decidedly less attractive towns. Situated at the apex of the Spencer Gulf it was buffeted by winds that carried either the red dust of the desert to the north or the sulphurous smoky pall from the power station to the south. Its position halfway across the continent also meant it was a place where all sorts of characters broke their journey to earn a little money on their way across. In those days, the Pepsi bottling plant and its staff were an unprofitable mess of low morale just waiting to be sorted out.

We spent the first month in the local hotel which was not a hotel as such but a drinking place with rooms upstairs. South Australia was one of the last states to lift the ban on drinking after six p.m., and in 1962 the 'six o'clock swill' was in full swing with workers crowding into the bars when they left work at five o'clock and staggering – or being thrown – out onto the pavement an hour later. My mother's reaction to the circumstance of living over a full-on pub was two-fold. Firstly, she retreated back into a sort of Englishness that had never been so pronounced; secondly, she had Toni and me spending a large proportion of each day strolling back and forth along the musty upstairs corridor with books on our heads repeating the vowels and such phrases as 'How now brown cow'. If that doesn't make sense to you, it doesn't to me either, but that was what happened and that was how we all survived those first weeks.

The house that came with the job was squeezed between that of the chief of police, a pleasant sort of fellow my mother liked immediately, and the Presbyterian minister, whom she did not, which fact is only important for what came later. More pressing was that prior to our arrival the house had been home to a kangaroo in addition to the previous human occupants. Had it not been fully carpeted some decades before, this may not have been so obvious. As it was, it stank. Badly. When the carpets were ripped up, out came the fleas in a mass that swarmed thickly onto my white socks. The dunny was at the back of an overgrown area that might once have been a garden. My father was sucked almost immediately into a host of difficulties at the rundown plant; we were put into the local high and primary schools respectively and my mother was left to make the best of things.

I believe she tried hard, the alien in that alien environment. She employed a woman to help and they scrubbed the house from the ceilings to the newly-sanded floors. She sewed curtains for the windows and matching bedspreads for the beds. She worked in the garden, cutting back the overgrown lemon tree, slashing at the long grass. There was no way, she said, that she was going to use an outside toilet, so a toilet and hand basin were installed in the sleep-out. She stood up to Pepsi, insisting that if she were required to put up with 'one of the worst sites in the country with heaven knows what rough types abounding' her teenage daughter be given a horse to keep her occupied and out of trouble. It could, she said, be stabled at the back of the factory where there was an area big enough for a lean-to stable and an enclosed yard.

A horse of my own. A real live horse of my own after all the riding lessons, the china horse collections, the story books, the Crown Jewel of my imagination; it was a literal dream come true.

But even through my fourteen-year-old preoccupation with self, it was clear to me that my mother was unhappy. From my own bout of homesickness, I recognised the bewildering mix of panic, anxiety and helpless longing. Sometimes it came winging in on the tail of one of the flimsy blue aerogrammes from Aunty Mon, catching her off-guard so she would disappear for her afternoon rest when I knew she was crying behind her bedroom door. Or she'd be lying on her bed listening to the cricket when I came back from school, the transistor radio gripped between her hands, her mouth tight. She was unhappy, yes, and I know Dad recognised this too. But she was a battler, and we believed that it was a matter of adjustment and that she would trade out of it.

It is only in looking back I can see that this longing for the life she had left behind had taken an even more ruthless hold on her than we could possibly guess: that she was engaged in battle with a form of melancholy as lethal as any cancer, a writhing, tangible thing that had crept up on her unawares and never really let go. However, the decision had been made to immigrate and as always money was tight; there was no hope of going back and little anyone could do about it. Counselling might have helped, but counselling back then – if available at all – was crude and psychotherapy more often than not took the form of shock treatment. Besides by now many of her friends were also leaving Kenya.

Some dropped down to central Africa, moving again to southern Africa in 1980 when Mugabe came to power in the new Zimbabwe. A few returned to England, others settled temporarily in Malaysia or Ceylon. Many finally found their way to Australia. Some stayed on in

East Africa – not many it's true, but some – and I think that had my mother been one of those, her story would have ended differently.

If coming from Nairobi to Port Augusta was a culture shock for my mother, it had its surprises for me, too, but not in quite the same confronting way. I lagged behind the Australians in just about every area: study, sport and growing up. The study I could handle: I had been at the rear of that field before and had caught up. Team sports I would never shine at, but I had always been a good swimmer. Growing up, which at that time meant being allowed to change the ankle socks for stockings and being permitted to wear lipstick, was more difficult. It set up differences between my mother and myself that had not been there before.

'At fourteen? Why on earth would you want to wear lipstick at fourteen?'

'Because everyone does and I feel left out. Besides, I'm nearly fifteen.'

'Lipstick,' she hissed. 'Do you know what lipstick's for. It's to attract boys. Is that what you want? At even *nearly fifteen*? You have your whole life ahead of you for that. Have you any idea how cheap that is?'

My mother was one step ahead of me, though, with the horse. Not long after this we drove out to one of the nearby stations in the foothills of the Flinders Ranges where my parents bought me a bright bay mare I named Gretel. My journal for 1962 had ended the day we docked in Sydney in May and this is the only other entry for that year. On October 19, I wrote: *My lifelong wish has been fulfilled. I have got a horse at last. I am now going down to the Bank to get ten pounds transferred into Dad's account for the saddle which I am paying for myself ...* What surprises me now is that I had as much as ten pounds in savings!

On the way home from a ride one day, I saw a dog lying in the gutter halfway between our driveway and next door. I slipped off my pony, knelt down by the dog to find it was dead. When we went to bury it, it had disappeared. Next day, there were two more, one dead, one still writhing, blood pouring from its throat. I rushed into the house.

'Mum. There's another dog in the gutter, not yet dead. Quick. Come quickly.'

I was crying too hard to see what was immediately clear to her.

'It's been shot. See? There's nothing we can do for the poor fellow. But …' her lips tightened as she looked towards the minister's house, 'I suspect I know what's happening. He's got a bitch on heat penned up in the back there. I've heard her yowling. That's why the dogs are coming around. We can't help the ones already dead, but we *can* stop him shooting any more. We can do something about that. Wait here. No. No, come with me.'

She strode up the path, thumped on the door. You could tell there were people inside, it had that feel about it, but the door didn't open. Her chin snapped up. 'All right. We'll try it this way then.' And she marched back the other way past our home to the policeman's house. This time the door opened and she had a long and progressively heated conversation with our other neighbour who made quite clear his reluctance to interfere.

'I can't believe it,' she fumed that evening. 'I just can't believe the police won't do anything.'

But this was a country town and she was an outsider, so things weren't any different really from any village situation anywhere in the world since the beginning of time. Nothing changed: each time the bitch came on heat, dogs died.

From the dust, the unaccustomed scrubbing and possibly the angst, she got a dermatitis that covered her hands. Small white bumps appeared over her fingers and around her nails that itched impossibly and distorted her fingers.

None of the Cortisone creams she was prescribed seemed to help and the irritation was constant, night and day. She covered her hands in Vaseline, put on white cotton gloves, gritted her teeth and waited out the long nights. I didn't guess then that the dermatitis was symptomatic of something deep inside her.

Port Lincoln

Meanwhile, Dad turned that plant around. As well as a good manager, he was a marketer and innovator. Pepsi took up many of his ideas – including, incidentally, his suggestion to PepsiCo International in the US head-office that the word 'Cola' be dropped from the brand name; the plant began to make money and in three years, he was rewarded with a transfer to the infinitely more desirable town of Port Lincoln, the fourth plant he had managed for Pepsi.

There they built their own house and had a good circle of friends. They both took up tennis and played in the Pennant league. Once again they were enjoying their lives, until suddenly and quite without warning, Pepsi appointed someone else as manager and Dad was out of a job.

My father was not a man to bear a grudge. But that hurt him. A lot. And no explanation was ever given.

Perth

In the West, he had a contact in an old friend from East Africa and the possibility of another job, so they sold the house and moved to Perth.

Once again, what followed were many moves – from the tumble-down asbestos shed in someone's backyard I shared with my father while my mother stayed behind to sell the house in Port Lincoln, to a flat owned by a madman who collected clocks and who flew out of his top-floor flat every time anyone closed a door, to a two-bedroom house they bought on a main road in a somewhat godforsaken suburb.

And again, there was little money to start with. But by then I was nineteen with my own job and an old (rather unreliable) Ford and I shared both the pay check and the car until they were back on their feet again. Dad's promised job finally eventuated and meanwhile my mother took a secretarial course, more for the promised contacts than the shorthand, and very shortly was offered a job as receptionist for a firm of West Perth accountants. Like everything she did, she did so well that it was not long before she was regarded as a public relations asset to the firm, which fact they recognised and rewarded.

My parents' last home together in the Perth Hills, they built largely themselves – calling it *Biowna* (by owner) – and carving the garden out of an acre of land. My mother worked shifts in the city, arriving home towards midnight to Dad waiting up for her with hot milk and nutmeg.

She had a new job as telephonist/receptionist for the ABC in Perth, and at last she was back with her beloved switchboard. Travelling back late one night, she was followed by a car which tried to run her off the road. Unfazed my mother memorized the licence number and Dad traced the man to his address and had a word or two with him. But after that, they decided she would wear one of Dad's old trilby hats as disguise when she drove back up to the Hills on her late-night shifts.

My mother, myself

My relationship with my mother was complicated – not unusual for a primal relationship – but exacerbated because of the degree of complexity of her own personality. Because of the relentless moving from house to house and place to place, our small family was a tight-knit thing which demanded a greater trust and perhaps generated a greater reliance on each other than normal.

As I've said, she was a woman undaunted by danger; in fact, she almost sought it out. She was a chancer, game for anything – always hatching some plan or the other, like going to Andamooka, living in a cave, mining opals and making a fortune (see the character in my short story **The Gambler**). She had a deep empathy for people and animals. She was a snob who abhorred snobs, who looked down her nose at social climbers. Although she was not a beautiful woman, she was attractive, an unashamed flirt who knew how to attract men. Africa reached out to something that went deep; it soothed the wildness inside her, compensated for something missing in her dreams of who she was or what she might become. Perhaps she named me Tangea after the glamorous spy in a novel she read because – as her first child – she projected onto me a life she would have chosen for herself.

One of her idols – among an eclectic selection of master painters, poet laureates, great musicians and film stars (the only common characteristic being that they reached the acknowledged top of their chosen professions) – was Coco Chanel and the timeless elegance she represented. In the early years, Mum dreamed up designs for her dresses and made her own newspaper patterns. And then, as they became more readily available in the obscure posts we found ourselves, she bought the flimsy tissue-paper patterns of Vogue, Simplicity and Butterick, sometimes combining them, knowing exactly what she wanted from each. As kids in Moshi, we watched Dad tape her up from neck to knee like an Egyptian mummy, apply a couple of coats of some hardening solution – and when it was dry enough, cut the structure carefully up the backbone until she could step out. This shell of her body was mounted on the stand he had made for it and used for her dressmaking. She might have been a fashionista on a budget – but she was so skilled a seamstress, so obsessed about having the right length hemline and so particular about how she presented herself to the world – you would never know it. She once told me that she would have loved to have been a wartime ambulance driver – certainly she knew how to meet crisis with calm – but given recognition of her dressmaking talent early enough, she might well have sat alongside the Chanels of her era. (Think "Tilly" played by Kate Winslet in *The Dressmaker* and you'll have a good idea of my mother and her style of grit.)

But above all, I remember her working: the sewing, yes, but also the unceasing packing and unpacking, the cleaning and painting, the gardening, the continual scraping together of money. I remember her agitation one Christmas in Tororo when we returned from compulsory long leave in England. The cold she hated had settled on her chest as pneumonia which quickly turned to pleurisy, but she was not concerned about herself – her distress was that there was no money for Christmas presents for Toni and me.

On the one hand she had this terrific sense of fun – we could laugh ourselves silly at a bus stop or in a café – on the other she had this locked-in sadness she was unable to shake off. Our mother was one mother to me, another to my sister. As my Aunt Ruby had said, she was 'wild' in that she lived life with a certain lack of restraint and, until the eve of leaving Africa, a lack of fear. In many ways, each of her children had the best and worst of her.

The seagull

I was away in those later years, married with children of my own, ricocheting from place to place just as my parents had done – South Africa, the U.K., the United States, Saudi Arabia, Hong Kong – returning to Perth from time to time. So it was Toni who took the brunt of the disease that never really let our mother go.

It was 1979 and I had been in Hong Kong for five days when my father phoned to say she was in hospital. 'We didn't want to worry you unnecessarily, dear,' he said. 'But your mother's not well. In fact, she's in hospital.' My husband John worked on getting me the first available flight; I mentally flew the plane, raced through the airport and sped to Royal Perth Hospital to find she was already in a coma.

'She can still feel, though,' said the young nurse. She pushed a needle under a red-painted nail and my eyes filled with tears as I watched my mother flinch. My mother's hands. My mother's beautiful nails. Have you ever had tears which flow like a waterfall inside you, but on the outside you look like one of those motionless golden statues in the street?

She died a few days later, and her body was cremated as she had requested: her ashes scattered over the roses at the University of Western Australia.

Just a week after I'd left I was back in Hong Kong to unpack, sort out schools, books, uniforms for the children, find a job, make new friends – just as my mother had done time and again.

Not long afterwards, travelling to work on the Star Ferry across Hong Kong harbour, a wingbeat to my right made me glance up. To one side of the ferry – so close I could see its eyes, the muscles in its wings – was a seagull. It flew alongside the boat to the landing stage, hovered for a few moments and then flew away. Not saying. But I just wonder. I felt better, more at peace, after that.

Lucky to be alive

We met up with some friends of my parents at a recent gathering. My mother’s fight to adjust came up.

‘She made a good fist of it,’ I stated.

‘No,’ my sister Toni contradicted flatly. ‘She didn’t. She didn’t at all.’

On her death certificate it says our mother died of a brain aneurysm at the age of sixty. There’s a biblical term used most often in the book of *Genesis* where after all the begetting there’s a fair number of souls that ‘give up the ghost’. Perhaps my sister was right. Perhaps in a slow, drawn-out way our mother had died and turned to straw that day on the Fremantle wharf when she stood looking back across the ocean. Perhaps she had simply left her heart behind.

But her life may not have turned out any better had she stayed. As my South African friend wrote, ‘To leave or not to leave? It’s not so simple.’

SMOKE IN MY EYES

A part of me knows that the sign hanging from the ceiling halfway down the pale green hospital corridor is not written in black blood with a paintbrush from Ali Baba's, that it was not set in place specifically to play games with my mind and that neither is it flapping crazily backwards and forwards. If I stopped – which I'm not going to do – I would see a plain black sign with bland white lettering designed to conceal its not-so-bland message, and I would observe that it hangs from steel stalks which are rigid and which are therefore not destined to flap. To fall, maybe. But not to flap. Ever.

According to the sign, this is the "Sleep and Mental Disorders" ward. It disturbs me that my father has been moved to this part of the hospital. I must remember to ask why on my way out. Close to a century in age he may be, but to the best of my knowledge Dad has never had a problem with either his sleep or his mental faculties. For example, when he came around from his hip operation a couple of weeks ago, he wanted to make my sister Prime Minister of Australia and my husband Treasurer. When I had asked, 'What about me?' he fingered his chin and squinted at the ceiling.

I worry about what might have taken place in the two days since my last visit. Which leads me to ask myself why you would couple sleep with a mental disorder? Does the fact that I'm temporarily confused by a simple sign coupled with my poor sleeping habit mean something more ominous lies ahead? Or is it simply that this is a catch-all ward for everything from bed-wetting to immobility, and something more creative than A – Z and shorter than a short story has to go on the sign?

I round the corner to Room 3B – twin beds, neither occupied. He might be in the shower or having an x-ray. Or even outside in the gardens on such a lovely day. Or maybe I have the wrong room. But no, the chocolate wrapper on the bedside cabinet against the far wall makes it very likely this is my father's bed. I duck out again, fall into step with a nursing sister pulling an oxygen cylinder and carrying a kidney-shaped dish in her other hand.

'He might have gone to the toilet,' she says. 'Or you could try the Rec Room. They often go there in the mornings. He might be grabbing a cup of coffee. Down the other corridor. Back the way you came.' Without altering her stride, she turns her head to gesture with her chin.

The Rec Room sounds vaguely racy. So does grabbing a coffee. I could do with one myself. Memories surface of the recreation room at a nursing hostel where we got up to all manner of things that could be linked to recreation – none of them dull.

But not this Rec Room. Or not today anyway. It is certainly large enough – could fit a snooker table or two in here and still have room for the tables and chairs dotted around. At the far end, dominating the room, is a poster of a kitten with the exhortation: *Smile. Tomorrow is another day*. Two larger tables in the centre make a sort of L-shape and there's Dad in a wheelchair slumped over the shorter one. The only other person in the room is a much younger man who is sitting at the end of the other table, drumming his fingers and staring at Dad while my father glares at the pile of building blocks in front of him, the kind sporting the coloured letters of the alphabet that you remember from two or three years of age.

In greeting, my voice comes out too high and bright, as if someone's plucked the wrong chords. I bend to kiss him and he raises his head. He looks up at me and down at the blocks. His lips curl downwards.

'Those don't look like a hell of a lot of fun!' I drop into a chair at his side, gently sweep them to one side. 'Coffee?'

He lifts his head again. Wet on the end of his lashes. Stupid Dad. I love him. 'Coffee? That what they call it?' he says.

'Tea then? How about it. And then maybe …' My gaze rests on a board and dice on the next table. 'Well, how about snakes and ladders? Remember how we used to play?'

I'm not sure we did. If we played anything, it would have been monopoly, except taking wild financial chances with a possibility of failure on the throw of the dice never was his thing.

It's a wild chance now, though. No point in asking him how he is. I don't need a degree in mental disorders to see he's thoroughly depressed. There's a cooking show blaring away on the television in the corner. The chap across from us hasn't stopped staring and drumming. I wonder whether he's in for sleep or for the other alternative. Dad stays grim and silent.

I set up the board with its counters and the dice and step across to the kitchenette to plug in the kettle. 'Tea?' I ask the other man. 'Or coffee maybe?' He shakes his head. Obviously Lipton's and Nescafé aren't a big hit here. But me, I need it. And Dad probably does, too. I think of the care with which he sets out the fragile cups and saucers of his beloved Shelley tea set when I visit him at home. Too bad, the sad irony in breaking a hip at the age of ninety-eight by doing the gentlemanly thing of stepping back to let someone pass in the street and stumbling over the kerb. I wash the mouth stains off the thick mugs and make his tea strong and milky, my grandmother's recipe for shock.

Mugs at our elbows, I remember the cake, the fruit cake I've made to his mother Eileen's favourite recipe. Wrapped carefully in aluminium foil. The other man's gaze switches from Dad to the cake and he runs his tongue over his lips. Dad glances his way for the first time and casually circles his arm around the little package. I feel embarrassed.

Men and sweet stuff. I think of the rest of the cake sitting cosily in its tin at home; I should have brought more because, from the way Dad is unwrapping this, he's not going to be into sharing. He's going to take his time over it, too.

I shake and throw the dice, first for Dad, then for me, and we progress in this manner, with Dad refusing to move his counter, but watching the game nonetheless between alternate sips and bites. Each time he breaks off a piece of cake he looks directly at the other man. Then his counter arrives at the head of a snake and he refuses to go down. I put the snakes and ladders to one side with the blocks, find the remote for the television and change the channel. Boxing.

'Blood sport,' says Dad. 'Silly fools.'

The man's gaze is still fixed on what's left of the cake. He clears his throat. 'Would you mind if I had the silver paper?'

Now it's our turn to stare. I speak for us both. 'Of course.' Still feeling awkward, I hop up to get a small plate, transfer the remaining piece of cake, shake the foil free of crumbs and pass it along the table. Dad is clearly upset by the boxing. I flick through the channels. 'Well, then, our choice is either these guys cooking or Sesame Street?' Nobody votes and I turn off the television.

With something to do with his fingers, the man changes. There's a light in his eyes and he is smoothing, twisting, shaping the foil. A boat, I think, or a miniature pirate hat.

'Used to be with the SAS,' he says. Bearing in mind the ward he's in, I nod politely. But he's on a roll. 'Most people think the SAS is all to do with fighting when it's more intelligence, peacekeeping. At the same time I could tell you stories that'd raise your hair. Who dares wins. Mind if I smoke?' He is smiling. The foil is equally transformed. It sits in front of him – a small triangular ashtray.

His hand firmly around his cake plate, Dad is looking on in amazement. I shrug. Both my parents had smoked, regularly given it up, smoked again. 'Go ahead.'

The SAS man taps his top pocket and flicks out a cigarette, takes a silver lighter from the inside of his waistband. We both watch as he lights up. He closes his eyes for a moment, draws in the smoke long and slow, turns his head to blow it away.

Manoeuvres, rescues, accidents, training. His legs stretched out, he leans back in his chair, talks and puffs, taps the ash into his little silver tray. In one of his stories he's in bed with a woman in a Chinese hotel when the police bust down the door. It's at this point that Dad senses the balance of my attention is no longer in his favour. He takes a last bite of cake and, employing his usual strategy, starts to cough. I hand him his mug. 'Have a sip.'

Dad's face starts to turn red. The SAS man stops talking. This time the crumb is well and truly lodged and there's only one thing that works when Dad has a true coughing fit. He's never been a drinking man, but a shot or two of brandy relaxes his larynx and fixes the problem. I know he has a small flask in his wet bag.

'Hang on,' I say. 'Back in a tick.'

Back in his room, I tug at the door of the bedside cabinet to find it locked. I press the alarm button, get ready to sound a high alert, but there's a nurse already on her way in. And she has a key. Agonising seconds before I have the flask in my hand, seconds more before we're back in the Rec. Dad's face is starting to turn purple and the nurse uses her intercom. I put the flask to his lips and as we hover over him, we're joined by the ward sister. Another minute and Dad has recovered enough to close his own hand around the silver flask and he starts to breathe instead of gasp.

I step back, let out my own breath in little spurts. The sight of the SAS man calmly puffing away and Dad swigging the brandy tickles an old party memory. I put my hands on my hips and – partly from relief and partly because the Rec Room no longer looks so stark, childish and incredibly cold – throw back my head and start to laugh.

'Just like the old times in Hong Kong!'

The ward sister has her hand on Dad's shoulder. She looks up at me, goes to smile and then her gaze lengthens as she takes in the other person in the room. The colour leaves her face and her mouth drops open. 'Is that man *smoking*?' She nudges the nurse. 'Quick.'

In tandem, they descend on the SAS man. One snaps the cigarette from his hand, stubs it to shreds in his ashtray, screws up the foil and drops it in a flip-top bin by the sink. The other confiscates the makings of any future smokes. He sits stiffly while he's frisked, his fingers drumming on the Formica until they suggest he get ready for lunch. A minute or two later, he follows them out of the room as Dad raises one eyebrow, purses his lips and stares down the room at the kitten poster.

Later, on my way out, the same nursing sister is at the duty desk and I stop to thank her for her quick response and to ask why Dad has been moved to this particular ward.

'That's what we're here for.' She smiles. 'As for your father, nothing wrong with him. Just needs a few more days to get used to his walker.'

'But why is he here?' I point upwards to the Sleep and Mental Disorders hanging from the ceiling.

'Oh, short of beds in Orthopaedic, that's all. He might be a bit down, but that's normal after an anaesthetic at his age. That'll fix itself as the drugs wear off. Hopefully.'

I don't like the 'hopefully', but let it pass. 'Just one other thing. That man at the other table. The one who was smoking. I feel a bit guilty. He was enjoying himself so much and I sort of spoiled his fun. Couldn't he be allowed to smoke outside?'

'What other man? Smoking?' She shakes her head. 'When?'

'Today. In the Rec Room earlier. You know? Where Dad had his turn.'

'No, I'm afraid I can't recall. There's no one I've come across smoking inside for a while now. Against the rules. They're allowed outside, I suppose, but we don't encourage that either. I can't say I remember anyone else in the room.'

'But there was,' I insist. 'Can you come with me for just half a minute? Please?' This is something that's easier to demonstrate than explain.

She sighs, follows me to the Rec Room. The L-shaped arrangement in the centre of the room is just as we left it, but the rest of the room has been tidied in the meantime – the mugs washed and stacked and the tables wiped clean of the taint of ash and crumb.

But the bin … I flip the top and to my relief it hasn't yet been emptied. I breathe out as my hand closes around the ball of silver foil still sitting on the top. I watch her face as I untangle it. And then, as I go to hold up the evidence, I see that the foil is empty. I look up to find her observing me carefully.

I turn to go home. Already I miss Dad. Mum, too. All of a sudden, smoke in my eyes.

‘WHAT’S THIS THING CALLED SEX?’

BUNTY’S STORY

I got to know Bunty because of Dad. Reacting in shock the day after Mum died, he had put their house on the market. To his surprise – and stirring up a further depth of grief when he realised he couldn't share the good news with the woman who'd helped him build it – their home sold for the asking price a day later.

That same weekend we – my sister and I – helped him move from the Hills down to South Perth – to a rather boring ground-floor flat, but it had the advantage of being one street back from the river with the convenience of shops, cafés and a second-hand bookshop across the street. And, although we didn't know it then, living in the penthouse of that block of units was Bunty whose husband George had recently died, a circumstance that had occasioned a move similar to Dad's some months before.

I was away from Perth for the next six years, living in Hong Kong and travelling back to Perth to see my father once or twice a year. Dad had written that he'd met Bunty and on one of my trips back he introduced us. She was a friendly uncomplicated woman – a pragmatist, as she often stated – and at that time, because numbers play tricks, she was twice my age. She was always beautifully dressed with heels, elegant fitted skirts and a brooch. And she always wore a wig. Bunty could make me feel very young and very naïve, although I was neither; other times she made me feel her age and her equal. She was, I realise now, more than friend, sometimes a mother, sometimes an elder sister.

Dad was the cementing factor in our friendship in those early days and he spent a lot of time up in her penthouse. Largely the way it went, I think, was that Bunty talked while Dad dozed. But she also cooked regularly for him, they played golf together, he partnered her a couple of times a week at bridge and they expanded their circle of mutual friends. Back in Hong Kong, every so often I would receive a letter from her with – as a postscript – a little bulletin: *Your father's looking very well* or *Your father's deteriorating*. Theirs was a solid friendship over a number of years but there was no doubt she had intentions that went beyond golf and bridge.

But on my next trip back to Perth, I can't say I found Dad fading. Not in the least. His hair was a lot longer than I remembered, but then it had always been thick, and it suited him silvery and curling on his collar. He had long fine fingers and his nails were neatly trimmed as usual. He seemed a little taller with a healthy colour to his skin. Certainly not frail and very much younger-looking than his seventy-six years.

That night I found a little note pinned to my pillow. *Have a lovely holiday darling. Lots of love Thekla.* I returned to the lounge holding out the piece of paper.

'Dad? Who on earth is this from? Who's Thekla?'

He glanced up briefly, flapped the pages of the newspaper he was reading.

'Thekla? Oh yes, Thekla. She's the lady … hmm … she comes to help me with the flat. Every fortnight, you see. Your sister arranged it for me.'

'But this? This seems … sort of well, very nice … from someone I haven't yet met.' It wasn't quite what I wanted to say, but my words fell into a sort of void due to the not-for-discussion manner in which my father was rattling the paper, shuffling his feet.

When I next flew back to Perth, Bunty was in the local hospital undergoing a series of tests for cancer. She was sitting outside in the sun when my father and I arrived to visit, pulling up chairs to sit beside her. Never very good at picking the right moment for such things, it was then that Dad chose to tell her he was moving in with Thekla. It wasn't so much that the look on Bunty's face changed, it was more the way her hand shot up to check her hair that expressed her dismay. In the uncertainty of that moment, her searching fingers knocked off her wig; she swung swiftly sideways to retrieve it and her chair toppled over.

Dad moved in with Thekla shortly afterwards and a year or two later they were married. She didn't play golf or bridge or love dogs but she was pretty and thirty years younger than he. And although Dad had always been a sucker for pretty women, his instinct was right and she proved a caring and constant wife and companion over the next quarter-century. But it was not until my father was out of the picture that my relationship with Bunty became a friendship in its own right.

By this time I had moved back to Perth and we fell quickly into the habit of meeting every fortnight at the lovely old UWA House, a place that mixed solemnity and grace with a friendship and sincerity that reminded me of the famous Ghurkha Club in Hong Kong. I remember asking her during one of those lunches how she came to be called Bunty and it's only now I realise she didn't actually answer my question. Instead she told me she'd been christened Anna Elisabeth. What a pretty name, I'd said. She rounded on me, her eyes glinting.

'Anna? It's perfectly horrible. Just imagine being called Anna. Anna!' She shuddered, and if she'd been low-brow, she might have spat.

She was born in the first years of the twentieth-century, the daughter of an English dentist, brought up by her grandparents, and the youngest of five or six sisters. Her first job was in a bank and she started stepping-out with George when she was sixteen or seventeen years old. It was between wars by then, they married and George was transferred to India where he managed a paint factory. It was on the ship out she met Peggy who was travelling to meet her own husband Keith and on this fateful trip a friendship was formed that would grow into a foursome and was to last all their lives.

Peggy was not only remarkably forthright for the era, but also a rather determined woman. They stood at the ship's rails on the approach to the Malabar Coast and, as the deck began to crowd, Peggy bent her head towards Bunty.

'I am concerned about something and I wonder whether you would explain it to me,' she whispered under cover of her hand. 'What's this thing called sex?'

It was not the question itself that surprised her, Bunty told me, but the fact that Peggy was married and yet still a virgin. She had gone on to explain the sex act as well as any Englishwoman of her time could manage to somebody who had been little more than an acquaintance a short while earlier.

Peggy had shaken her head vigorously. 'How absolutely ghastly. I certainly won't be doing *that*.' But dance she could and did; in fact, all four were adept dancers and there were many Saturday nights at the Taj Hotel in Bombay when the couples danced until the early hours. Partition came to India in 1948 and along with many other expats the couples dispersed: Peggy and Keith to return to England, Bunty and George to Australia.

In Perth, Bunty and George tried their hand at most things. They started by buying a tobacconist shop on the corner of what is now the Hay Street Mall; they had a fast-food bar; they bought an orchard, getting up before dawn to pick, pack and take the fruit to market. For a while they lived in the Hills along the Darling Scarp east of Perth where Bunty was postmistress 'swapping gossip' up at the local post office; when they moved down to the city, she made a good living from the property market.

She was well into her seventies when she bought two nursing homes which she managed with the help of an administrator. Although she had adored India and its lifestyle, she was pragmatic enough to know that it was a phase she had been lucky enough to experience and – and unlike my own mother – her realism saved her from spoiling the present by dwelling on the past. By the time George died they had been married for over sixty years and they had had only one serious argument in all that time. That was the time George put on his hat, left home and came back two days later. Bunty wasn't one to stir the pot with questions or recriminations and life continued just as happily as it had before. They didn't have children. 'Because somehow there was never time. We were enough for each other and quite happy as we were. But we always *talked*, you see, dear. That's the secret. To make a good marriage, you must *talk*.'

One day – she was nearly ninety years of age by this time – Bunty arrived at the new University House (somewhat grander than the old UWA House, but to my mind, rather sterile, lacking the atmosphere of the other) with something on her mind and she was never slow in coming to the point. As soon as we were seated with our plates of roast and two veg, she gave a measured glance around at the other tables to make sure, as she always did, that no one was close enough or concerned enough to listen in on the 'goss' and then she leaned towards me. She wasn't exactly agitated but the carefully blended colour on her cheekbones was augmented by something more.

'I've just had a letter from Keith,' she said. 'Peggy's died.' She looked down, took a sip of water. 'He's devastated, poor man. And he sounds exhausted, too. She was blind for the last ten years and he did everything for her. I wonder … I was wondering whether you think it would be a good idea to invite him out for a break, for a holiday?'

We debated the point. Having lost my own husband some years before, I was aware of the strangeness of death, of its ruthless finality, and of the time it can take to learn to live in the world again. But I also knew that my own experience was not universal and that everyone was different. Perhaps, we convinced ourselves, he would be very grateful for a change of scene. *Perhaps* it was just what he needed.

'You don't think he might feel it's a bit forward of me, do you?'

I tried to put myself into the place of a man I had never met, tried to substitute the blue of the sky under which we were lunching for the pewter of English skies and to imagine the grim business of tidying up the fragments of life his wife had left behind. But without knowing the reality of his circumstances, it was impossible to guess what state of depression he might or might not be in. For all I knew, Bunty's gesture of friendship might well be a lifesaver.

'I don't think so. It's friendly, after all, isn't it? A friendly gesture with no strings. It's not as though there was anything between you besides friendship, was there?'

She hesitated. 'Once only,' she said. 'Only once – the four of us in a taxi. Peggy and George in front and Keith and me in the back. He put a hand on my knee. I wondered after that whether he would say something, would follow up on it at all. But do you know, he never did.'

It was several months before she received a rather agitated reply to her letter of condolence. She handed me the airmail envelope. No, he was unable to come out. In fact, that was the last thing on his mind. He missed Peggy. Badly. Maybe later. Meanwhile he was sure Bunty would understand. Bunty *did* understand on the one hand; on the other, she was rather quiet that lunch day. But the following Christmas they exchanged cards as usual and everything was back to normal.

It was not until spring of the following year that Bunty's good friends Anne and Stewart decided to visit England. They were going via Bombay and had asked Bunty to join them. That was enough for Bunty. She began to plan.

'And we'll have dinner at the Taj! It's still standing evidently. I wonder whether they've done it up, how it's changed. And how India's changed! And then onto England for nearly three weeks.' All her sisters but one had passed on and her circle of friends had long been restricted to Perth. But she had her own nieces and nephews and a niece of George's of whom she was particularly fond.

'Do you know it's getting on for seventy years since I've been back. Seventy years!' Her aquamarine eyes sparkled through the thick lenses. She might, she said, even drop Keith a line.

So she went to England, my ninety-year-old friend, and when she returned she called me.

'Quick, Tangie. Come round. I have lots to tell you.'

I arrived at her apartment, gramophone tunes from the war years greeting me at the door. She grasped me firmly and led me into the difficulties of a quickstep across her thick-pile carpet. Breathless, finally, she made us a pot of tea. She didn't just glow, she was *ablaze*.

'Listen,' she said. 'Let me tell you …'

When he heard she was coming, she said, Keith had invited her and her friends for afternoon tea.

'I thought it might be awkward,' she said. 'But it wasn't. We just talked and talked.'

Talked so much in fact that Anne and Stewart – either from diplomacy, boredom or both – decided to go for a drive. But by the time they returned a couple of hours later, the discussion hadn't abated in the least. In fact, by that time, Keith had invited Bunty to stay the night. Her friends left for their hotel; Keith opened a bottle of wine, cooked and served a meal and eventually they retired.

'It was a little while later and I was reading,' she said to me. 'There was a tap at the door. "Just about to turn in and wondered whether you've got everything you need," he asked. And I must say he looked rather smart in his paisley dressing gown. "Would you like more water? A different book perhaps?"

'"Oh, no. I've everything I need," I'd answered, putting down my book. "You've been most kind and I'm doing very well indeed. Very comfortable. Lovely evening altogether."

'"Yes, it was rather good," he said, advancing into the room. "Are you sure I can't get you something?"

'He sat on the edge of the bed and took my hand,' she said, her eyes very round. 'And then, well, you can guess the rest.'

She stayed with Keith for the next two weeks. Each night they had sex. Each morning he shooed her out of the house, settled her in the summer house with the morning paper and brought her breakfast. Once he had taken care of the housekeeping and prepared the evening meal, they went for drives. A different set of sites, a different pub or tavern for lunch each day.

Her eyes glowed as she described their outings. Bunty was in love, as swept away as any sixteen-year-old. It was ferocious, consuming and romantic.

Over the next couple of years she went back to England several times and each time she returned more radiantly beautiful than when she left. She would arrange to be wheeled onto the plane at Perth airport and wheeled off at Heathrow where Keith would be waiting. Each trip followed the format of the first, and the sex that Peggy had shunned during her lifetime only grew wilder and more abandoned.

It didn't matter that Bunty had only one breast, the other removed forty years before due to an unfounded suspicion of a cancerous growth. It didn't matter that under the wig her hair was sparse and white. Or that her lover was younger than herself. It didn't matter that there were only two single beds and narrow ones at that; they moved the two beds into one room and lashed the legs together to stop her falling through the gap. Keith had dispensed with both her nightie and her wig early on. She grinned. 'He literally ripped them off me and threw them across the room saying "You have absolutely no need of this nonsense."'

She started to talk of moving to England. And then one day the flimsy blue aerogrammes from Keith ceased. She tried to call, but the phone rang out. She made other enquiries, to no avail. Anne is a librarian and a sleuth researcher, but she too drew a blank. Unbeknown to Bunty, we also called Births, Marriages and Deaths. But Keith's name didn't show up. He had disappeared.

'Perhaps he's sold up and gone down to Devon to live with his brother. Perhaps the house got too much for him. He was talking along those lines. Or perhaps he's had a heart attack and he's in hospital. Or *perhaps* …'

In the end I could only do what a friend can do, and listen. I discovered that the sound, shape and intensity of heartbreak when you are ninety-three years of age is not much different from any age. It always hurts. Lots.

Another thing I learned was that being young or being old is both more and less than a date on a birth certificate. And that true friendship is not only capable of surviving the tangles of time and distance, but death itself.

IDENTITY

THE UNFOLDING JOURNEY

I'm in a synagogue for the first time in my life – in the semicircle of the top gallery, a theatrical space that juts out over the downstairs seating. In fact, all around me is theatre, something I enjoy in my infrequent visits to the Roman Catholic Church, but which surprises me along with so much else here in this Jewish place of worship.

All around me are gloriously coloured stained-glass windows, above me is a huge ornate dome and immediately below in the centre of the ground floor is a raised platform with benches, high counters, wooden railings. Two or three sets of shallow steps lead from this central podium to the long pews that range backwards across the ground floor to the outer walls of the building. At the front is another raised area, a sort of stage with heavy curtains as a backdrop, a small Juliet balcony above. There is a lot of wood, beautiful woods: the upstairs pews, counters and railings in English oak, down below Victorian ash, perhaps, and I suspect the central platform and railings are of the red gum that was first felled for use in the railway sleepers of early Melbourne.

I had started off the morning of this *bar mitzvah* ceremony downstairs in the small section of the male-only ground-floor space set aside for those of the female congregation who have difficulty with the stairs, so I could sit with my newly discovered cousin Rosetta and her mother Mena. But I had barely sat down when Rosetta urged me upstairs.

You will see much more from up there. Besides it's more fun, she'd said with a wink and a small smile.

She's spot on, of course. As the ceremony below me unfolds, I am quite frankly a little dazed. I had thought I'd feel like an interloper, a bit of a fraud, and had brought along my invitation in case I was challenged. But it's quite the opposite. Instead I have the feeling that I'm taking part in a play where I have a very small part as a member of the crowd scene, but a part nonetheless. Useless to attempt to take it all in at once. One of my first thoughts is: I must come back. To even begin to absorb this properly, I must come back. And I'd like to repeat this rare experience with my daughter and perhaps her daughter, too.

What strikes me next is the extraordinary combination of formality, informality and solemn ritual. The formal part takes place downstairs which, as I've said, apart from the one small area, is reserved for men. The men folk sit shoulder to shoulder, all with neat black, grey or braided caps on their heads and most wear shawls draped across their shoulders – cream-coloured with a distinctive thick black stripe. Although there is a considerable amount of coming and going, in between they sit quietly.

But where downstairs the mood takes its cue from the sombre colours of dress, upstairs it's great deal more riotous. Rosetta is not wrong: given that we're all here for nearly three hours until midday, it could also be more fun. The invitation said 9 a.m., but it's 10 o'clock and still people are wandering in. Those in the know get there later, we had learned at the Shabbat dinner the night before when Rosetta had outlined what to expect, what to do and what *not* to do during the *shule* ceremony. On no account wear trousers; and women *can*, but don't have to wear a hat, she'd said. As it turns out, about half wear hats or fascinators, no trousers, but skirts of all lengths in bright colours like a box of Smarties. Almost all of them chatter. And when they finish talking to one person, they get up, move across to someone else and start over. Occasionally one of the older women will openly shush or hold a finger up to her mouth; sometimes a louder 'ssh' drifts up from downstairs.

But the busiest space of all is that of the central raised platform down below (that I later learn is the *bimah*) where there are several people milling around and taking turns to read, chant or sing, a constantly changing tableau. It's a double ceremony here today – a *bar mitzvah* as well as banns for a marriage to take place in two weeks' time.

In a relatively recent twist to my own life, the young man celebrating his *bar mitzvah* is Rosetta's grandson Jamie, and thus related to me in the complex way these things work. He sits patiently on a bench in the *bimah* in between his recitals of the *Torah.* A young girl of perhaps three or four years of age dressed in a bright pink t-shirt and tulle skirt sits on the high reading counter behind him, looks out towards the congregation, swings her legs against the railings. I spot my husband in the cap he had been given as a present the night before sitting quietly against the far wall, completely absorbed in the text he is reading.

It's a recent relaxation of the rules – this one that allows the women to sit downstairs – says a woman called Anna, who drops down from the row above to sit beside me and who, along with informing me apropos of nothing that it's the face and hair that are important for a woman and who cares about the figure, fills me in on the spectacle unfolding below.

It's been some years since she was last here, she tells me, in between trying to attract the attention of Jeremy, Jamie's father, who sits in a front pew and keeps a close eye on his son, getting up from time to time to lend his support. Jeremy is her cousin, she tells me, and they grew up together like brother and sister. I realise then that she, too, is related to me in some configuration, since her cousin Jeremy is Rosetta's son. In fact, half the people who are crammed wall-to-wall in this building are related to me. Jeremy acknowledges her wave with a smile and she relaxes back onto the bench. How lucky they are, I think. Lucky to have each other, to have this wide and encompassing relatedness – and how lucky I am to have stumbled into their midst.

So I relax too, smile into the enormity of the elaborate dome above me and wonder whether my father had ever entered a synagogue and what he would say if he could see me now. And how my grandfather would feel. The St Kilda *Shule* was built over 140 years ago; he would have sat just underneath where I am sitting. I can feel it. And yet I had known nothing about this entire branch of my family until a few years earlier.

I was too busy being a wife, mother and establishing a career to think much about identity for the first forty or so years of my life, although it was clear I was a long way from fifth-generation anything. I had a mother who prided herself on her Englishness, but who wouldn't be parted from her Kenyan passport. My father was Australian, with an Australian-born father and an Irish mother. I've had lots of surnames stretching from my birth name of Coton – which many people spelled (and most pronounced) as Cotton – to other surnames that came my way along with husbands one, two and three.

If there was a norm in those first four decades of my life, it was the wandering – a rootless roving that inevitably led to a plethora of addresses, countries, continents. In fact, by my teen years, packing up and moving on had become almost routine. We were a small family in those nomadic years – my mother, father, sister and me – a tight nucleus moving from one house or suburb or country to another as one cell. Although I didn't know it then, it was going to take half a lifetime for me to shed my habit of moving on and to begin to realise the critical nature of identity.

In fact, for a long time I was quite proud of what I came to call my *rootlessness*, first writing about it in an article published just after my daughter was born. The point I was trying to make was that I was like a cactus with roots so shallow that moving – or uprooting – was painless and therefore my home was and would forever be wherever I found myself. Brave words, I think to myself now. Brave and not quite stupid, but not thought through either and all part of the confusion of those years. One of my memories is of a check-out queue at a London supermarket where the woman scanning my groceries glanced up briefly. 'And where do you come from?' she asked. She was after a simple answer, I think, a single word dropped in somewhere between ringing up the price of a tin of baked beans and a quarter-pound of butter. When I replied, 'Africa and India', she stopped to gaze at me. 'Well, you don't look either African or Indian,' she said, which led to my explanation that I was born in one and had just come from the other, while the line behind me began to sigh and shuffle.

It was in the dizzy months after my second husband died that identity first became important. It dawned on me that part of the price you pay for rootlessness is a somewhat shaky hold on your sense of self along with the friends and addresses you leave in your wake.

Do you know that if you don't have a clear motherland, some place where you were born and grew up with scads of cousins and groups of schoolmates who become adult friends and with whom you can discuss most things because you've known each other forever – do you know that if you don't have that, your idea of yourself can be unformed, unclear, a bit misty, like a ghost that feels but has no centre? At that point, that's what it was like for me and I often wonder how it is for others who have lived their lives in transit.

I suddenly felt the need to list the address of every place I'd lived from birth to the present day. And they needed to be *bona fide* addresses, I decided – places where I'd lived long enough to get my mail sent to a valid address instead of the *poste restante* I'd used countless times, including the year I was pregnant with my first child when I set up house on three different continents in the nine months between her conception and birth.

I suppose the database was a way of taking stock at this murky junction of my life. I was no longer particularly young, but neither was I old. I had been divorced for some time from my children's father and was now recently widowed. My children were by then in their late teens, pushed by my own crises into an early fledging. In some strange way, the lists were a way of discovering parts of myself from the routes – both geographical and metaphorical – that I had taken to arrive at this rather disoriented point. Like a chameleon, I felt I had taken on the colour and essence of my surroundings in exchanging parts of myself with the places and the cultures I had lived in and with. Maybe I was the same outwardly, but I was certainly different within. And in this way, or so I thought at the time, the list not only charted the roads I had taken, but also pointed to the way ahead.

So by now I was forty years old and I'd had sixty-three addresses, gone to ten different schools and lived in countless states and countries on five different continents. In one of these houses I had lived for a record five years which upped the ante in terms of the number of changes that took place in the other years. The upshot of the list was a rebellion against change – impotent and ultimately useless – but at least it led to a degree of awareness, a message to myself to stay put, make friends and gather a deep bed of moss.

My concept of identity firmed in the years I spent researching my PhD. When I started on this project I'd completely missed what would become the focal point of my own hypothesis. It was not until I began to write up the thesis that I realised all five writers I had chosen to illustrate my enquiry into orientalism had their own identity issues. And that a by-product of the thesis would be an unwrapping of the ideology of culture and philosophy of self.

It was at this point, when I was just beginning to feel I had the whole issue of my own identity done and dusted, that it split wide open at a deep rich seam.

But Anna is talking again. She points out her mother in the row in front of us and, on cue, the mother turns and smiles. Her mother is remarried, she says, as is she herself, and she points out their husbands, both sitting towards the back of the synagogue. My husband in his brand-new black cap is sitting close by. Anna is waving, so I wave too. But Richard is still riveted to the text he has in his hands. At the time, I think perhaps this covers an uncertainty on his part or a hint of shyness, but later he tells me he was reading the story of Lot who hid in a cave with his teenage daughters after the destruction of his hometown of Sodom and the turning of his wife into a pillar of salt. Bereft of male company, the daughters get their father drunk, strip him naked and have sex with him – the only hope they have in the current circumstances of having children. The eldest daughter conceives and gives birth to a son which in some accounts leads to the line of which Jesus is a descendant. This is possibly my husband's first real reading of Genesis and from the expression on his face, it is clear he views the Bible – the Old Testament at least – in a whole new light.

It is at this point that an imposing figure of a man – very Moses-like with his long, white beard – stands to face the congregation. He is a visiting Rabbi to this synagogue to mark the importance of this occasion, Anna whispers. He is also a respected lawyer and an opera singer of some renown. He starts to sing and his voice explodes, circling the building, climbing up past pews and people to spread into the upstairs layer, and then to the dome, rising, tumbling, circling, rising again, freewheeling like welcome swallows on the wing. Afterwards Jamie recites from the Torah in Hebrew, the chant spiralling high and clear into the void left by the ringing tones of the opera singer. There are a couple of young women circling the upstairs area carrying baskets of gaily wrapped sweets. Anna takes a handful, nudges me to do the same.

We wait until Jamie's ceremony is over, she murmurs, and then we throw these at him. Try to hit him. For luck.

A little while later, Jamie recites again and then he is through. Handfuls of sweets fly from the top floor, one or two score a hit, most are bad shots. The little girl in her bright pink tutu slips from her high perch on the reading counter of the *bimah* and the ground floor comes alive with children scrambling for sweets – for all the world like the young boys I remember diving for silver coins in the seas off Gibraltar. Jamie looks on from the elevated position of his coming of age. He is thirteen years old and this ceremony is to celebrate his entry into adulthood. Impossible to tell whether he regrets the passing of the days when he too scrambled for sweets. He and two members of the family move towards the stage-like platform at the front of the synagogue, stand facing the congregation on either side of a heavy curtain.

What are they doing now? I ask Anna as I watch the scrolls of the Torah being reverently rolled together and inserted into a gold circular container, something like a giant mace, that the Rabbi places across his shoulder. He, too, steps towards the front of the tabernacle. The two men take hold of the bell pulls of the curtain.

See, Anna says. Now they open the curtains. That space behind, that niche, is called the Ark and that is where the Torah is stored. Traditionally the Ark faces in the direction of Jerusalem. And see that small balcony above the stage there? Until quite recently that was where the musicians played during the ceremony. It was lovely. But they don't seem to use it now.

Change. Changes everywhere. How did I get here, I wonder? In the middle of this new extended family that seems to go on forever. The night before we had been invited to 'a small family meal to meet the main players in tomorrow's ceremony – quite informal and we'll keep it brief as we have to be up early in the morning'. The small family meal turned out to be a Shabbat dinner for fifty adults plus children, a three-course, sit-down meal under chandeliers. How did I get here? Again, I gaze up at the dome.

About ten years ago, something that has been there all along comes rather suddenly to light. I am having a cup of coffee with my sister when she brings out a book she's taken from my own bookshelf at some point in the past.

'I've been meaning to return this,' she says passing me our grandfather's opus, *The Magic and Science of Jewels and Stones*. 'You know something, Tange? I think we're Jews.'

'Jewish,' I reply automatically. 'Don't be ridiculous.' To the delight of the people around her, Toni lives her life a little to the right of outrageous. She should have been an actress, not one of the most successful practitioners of alternative medicine in the country. But in a lot of things, she reminds me of our aunt, Dad's sister. She likes to shock. In a different way from Nan, but shock she does.

'No, really,' she says. 'Why don't you ask Dad.'

Dad lives in the country, ninety kilometres away in a town called York. Next time I visit, I ask him.

'This book of your father's. All these years. Crazy, but I never thought to ask. Why does he call himself Isidore Kozminsky? When you're Coton?'

'Oh that.' He waves his hand. Flaps the problem away. Dad should have been an actor, too. This flamboyant family. Am I the only one to miss out on the dramatics? But I persist.

'Yes. But Kozminsky? Coton?'

'Well darling. A long story. Just remembered there's some of that delicious quiche left in the fridge. Second shelf. Asparagus. Do you think we could warm up a little for lunch? The microwave … I'll show you how to use it …' and he levers his body out of his chair and starts towards the kitchen at a stooped half-run.

After lunch, I make coffee and use his best cups – which always pleases him – and I broach the subject again.

'Odd, suddenly,' I say. 'I always thought somehow that Isidore Kozminsky was your father's pen name and well …' But how honest am I being now? In spite of the decades the book has sat in one or another of my itinerant bookshelves, in spite of the number of times I've packed and unpacked it, beyond knowing it was written by my grandfather, have I ever given it much thought? To be honest, I don't think so. I think it's entirely possible that it was the last thing on my mind in all the moves, homes, countries, children and jobs – and the fact there was a link missing somewhere didn't even cross my mind. Because other than the pen name scenario, it didn't really add up.

But now my father is nearly ninety, my sister has opened a Pandora's box of possibility, and I want suddenly to know more. Dad – however – doesn't want to tell and, equally suddenly, does frail very well. So Toni is right and we're Jews – or we could be. The connection is close and the light is very bright.

Over the next few minutes, and then in small drifts in response to my questions over the next few years, the story comes out. Some of the story. In bits that later turn out to be completely out of context and still have names missing.

It takes me ten years to piece it all together, to realise the colourful bedtime stories of my childhood are in fact true stories with the names, dates and any relevance to our family of origin edited out. Deleted.

The piecing-together took place in spurts. In those years, my son Viv lived in Melbourne and his calls to a Kozminsky phone number led him to Mena whose first husband was Dad's cousin Geoffrey. Geoffrey was Dad's best friend while they were growing up together in St Kilda, his best man at his first wedding and the only Kozminsky my father would talk to after the 'family rift' which led to the name change and my father's subsequent and complete denial that there had ever been a time before. At the point of Viv's intervention, Mena and I began to correspond and that was the start of this whole new family of second, third and fourth cousins gradually filling the stage – a cast of players moving in from the wings after a performance.

Mena was writing her own family history and we emailed back and forth, exchanging family anecdotes, facts, certificates, anything and everything relevant to this family she had married into and the one that I was only now discovering I was part of. I had wanted to write the story of my great-grandmother Emma Solomon, the wealthy woman who had arrived on the docks in Melbourne around 1869.

You won't find anything, Dad reiterated every time I saw him. If anyone could have unearthed the truth of Emma's background it would have been my father, he says. And he tried. Believe me, he tried hard.

I don't doubt he tried, I reply, but these days there's so much more genealogical help available. It's a popular pastime to trace your roots. Times have changed. Circumstances that were regarded as shameful or those that needed to be hidden 150 years ago are treated somewhat differently today.

I look back and I'm ashamed of my certainty. Comparatively gentle though I felt it to be at the time, in retrospect my words have an echo of parent-bashing.

I spent days and then weeks in national archives and genealogical centres looking through handwritten shipping lists – some almost undecipherable, others in enviable Copperplate script – made many trips to Melbourne and one memorable trip to Mortlake and Buangor in country Victoria. In England we visited anywhere of possible relevance: cemeteries, the town with the name of Coton, St Catherine's House for records of Births Deaths and Marriages. It's quite amazing the number of banks with fires between certain critical years that wipe the records clean out of existence, heartrending to find an impressively bound book in an archive, the pages of which your white-gloved fingers turn with care only to find the page you're after has been so neatly sliced out you'd never know it was missing unless that was the particular page you needed to view.

And so Dad turned out to be right. All references to Emma had been wiped. Although there was one hell of a story in the rift that split apart one of Victoria's prominent settler families, it was to be Isidore who took centre stage, not his mother. It was nearly ten years later that this book – *A Break in the Chain: the Early Kozminskys* – was published that tells the story that leads directly to this point: to my gazing through the domed ceiling of the synagogue to the sky beyond where I'm asking my grandfather how he feels about my being here. A completely alien feeling – an almost-belonging – is gradually replacing that of the trespasser I'd felt myself to be.

Early fears of a completely opposite reaction from the one I received from Melbourne's Jewish population were gradually buried. On one trip to Melbourne, her arms around my waist and her head pressed into my breasts, Mena hugs me goodbye at the train station. We're family, she says. Her voice shakes with emotion. Family. Please always remember. She turns abruptly to follow her husband Bob to the car.

This newly discovered extended family has been so warm, so including and so sincere. On their side. Not Dad's. Never Dad's. I try to share Mena's emails with him, but he doesn't want to know. Turns his lips down. Makes a face. But he doesn't mind me writing the story. As the book progresses, I read out some of the scenes to him on my trips out to York and he rubs his hands together in the (Jewish) way he has: Yes, that's the way it was, darling. That's the way it was.

But by the time the book is complete – or as complete as I can make it – he is a few weeks short of his hundredth birthday. He is in hospital and I sit with him, take his hand. Dad, it's finished. I've finished the book. All I have to do now is find a publisher. He gives me a weak smile, returns the pressure of my hand, achieves a thumbs-up with the other. Sometime in the early morning of the following day, he stops breathing.

Technically, I guess, my sister Toni and I are not Jewish. Even if Emma were Jewish – and unsubstantiated anecdotes about our great-grandmother abound – the maternal line has been broken twice, first in our grandfather's marriage to an Irishwoman, secondly in that our own mother was not Jewish. But still, I would like to know for sure about Emma. My father swore that she was not Jewish and that 'there was no Jewish stuff there'. But my cousin Michael maintains the opposite. After the ceremony at the St Kilda *Schule*, Michael takes me to the foyer to point out a tablet mounted on the wall. My grandfather Isidore, his brother Michael and sister Minnie had donated twenty pounds back in the 1920s to have their mother Emma's name included on this commemorative tablet and Michael cites this example as incontrovertible evidence of Emma's Jewishness. No Rabbi in those days would have allowed a stone to commemorate a non-Jew to be placed on the wall of the synagogue, he says.

A few days after the *bar mitzvah* ceremony, I am addressing a small group of about twenty people as part of the Melbourne Jewish Festival, a Q&A session on my recent book. And although once again I'm nervous of the reception I might receive from the Jewish members, I need not have worried: as it turns out, they couldn't have been warmer or more involved. Again, the interest settles on Emma: whether or not she was a Jew. I tell them of the stone tablet in the synagogue foyer and repeat what Michael said to me about the Rabbi not allowing her name to be up there on the wall if she wasn't Jewish. Nonsense, says one of the Jewish women present. Rabbis, in that era particularly, would have been much too pragmatic to turn down a donation on the basis of whether someone might or might not have been Jewish.

But one question in particular resonates with me. The woman asking speaks slowly, as if she herself is considering. Just supposing, she says. Suppose you find out for sure that your great-grandmother Emma was Jewish, that her mother was a Jew. Wouldn't that make you a Jew? So how would you feel then?

For a moment I don't know what to say. Somehow the spoken question itself becomes more important than a debate about broken or unbroken maternal lines and the minute of silence is intense throughout the room. I feel a strange sense of responsibility to get the answer right: both for me and for the people in front of me.

A decade earlier when Toni first broached the possibility of our Jewishness, I was quite frankly shocked. The feeling that accompanied my reaction at that time was somewhat akin, I should imagine, to being told we had a sibling we didn't know about. Or that our parents weren't married. Big family-secret stuff. But several years later, when writing the draft of the postscript to the book, the way I phrased (and felt) the closeness of this Jewishness was like this: 'As the story took shape, I felt strange, as if I'd entered a world that was over-bright and a trifle uncomfortable'. In an earlier draft, I had likened this feeling to that of a chick being newly hatched.

But as I stare back at the audience in front of me, I remember the sense of *rightness* I'd experienced in the synagogue just a few days before – for the first time in my life, I'd had a glimpse of what it was like to belong.

There comes a type of clarity. After all the moving acts of kindness and the warmth shown to me by Mena and her family, I feel pride at being part of such a culture – and something deeper that I can't describe. But as to really *belonging*? As I step backwards, I wonder whether the words I ascribe to my grandfather in a passage from the book I read out earlier are really my own. Or whether this is something we shared. It's the part where my grandfather says:

'No one understands better than me the loneliness of never quite fitting in. Of always being neither one thing nor the other. But by being observant, by attending the synagogue, by marrying a Jewish woman, what would that achieve in terms of identity? Would that make me Jewish? Or would I still be on the outside? Not quite a Jew, but the man who married a Jew and had Jewish children?'

I can of course claim a double identity – but I suspect I won't. I suspect that whatever I do or however I feel, I will always be on the outside of both the Jewish and the non-Jewish sectors of society – welcomed by both, perhaps, and welcoming both, but not fully claimed by either.

So what I finally reply is just that. That I think whatever happens, I'll always be on the outside looking in.

Honest at the time, but in retrospect I'm angry with myself. Why do I have to be so prescriptive? Why do I have to *arrive* anywhere? Why not go with the ebb and flow of life? The natural moving forward, stepping back? Maybe identity is not something that is fixed, but always elusive, forever changing. Perhaps you never quite get there. Perhaps *I'll* never get there. Wherever *there* might be. My mind flicks back to one of the key characters that figured in my PhD thesis, specifically Leonard Woolf, the final volume of his autobiography, his message in the title of the book: *The Journey Not the Arrival Matters* that I made mention of in the introduction to this book.

Let go the certainties along with the confusion bound to follow. Burn the databases. Take joy in a sudden small smile of recognition as Anna did. Remember the tone of Mena's voice: We're family, we're family. The care Rosetta took to guide us in the ritual of the ceremony, and her words, I thank your book for bringing us together. Michael's jovial instruction as he kept my place in the chanting the evening before, his concern and generosity in passing on all he knows about the family to me. The warmth that surges through me when they call me 'cousin'. I would like to think that my grandfather smiles down from whatever heaven he has landed in.

But just how Dad would feel about all this, I'm not so sure.

ONCE WERE IMMIGRANTS

I WANT TO JOIN

A scrap of ruled paper, curling, edges furred as if torn against the edge of a ruler or a knife, arrives with the mail that evening. House help available. Energetic, reliable woman. Can do cleaning of all sorts. Also ironing or look after children. Call Shanta. It gives two phone numbers.

But when I try to call, the digitised voice on the landline tells me to re-read the number, to dial again more carefully. After several tries, it's obvious that it's either the wrong number or not yet connected. The mobile is turned off. I give up and slip the piece of paper into my erratic filing system from which much has been known never to re-emerge.

When I come across it just by chance a few days later, I try once more. This time the phone is answered and there is a male voice the other end of the line.

Yes?

Shanta? I'd like to speak to Shanta, please.

This is her husband. I am husband. Please tell to me.

I have some work for her. I may have some work. Can she call me please?

She will come to see you. The next night. Is all right?

Thursday? Yes that's fine. I give him my address.

On Thursday, around 6 p.m., there's a knock at the door and they are both there. Husband and wife. They follow me upstairs and I talk to him as either his English is better or he is her negotiator. He is dressed in khaki slacks with a white open-necked shirt, while she is clothed more traditionally, her folded arms tucked tight into an orange sari. A woman in her early thirties, she stands quite rigid, a slight frown on her face, her head held still, her eyes the only movement as she follows the conversation.

This is what I'd like help with. This brass and copper cleaning, some silver. I have lots of pots and planters. As you can see. Does she, does your wife, know how to do this?

He shrugs. I can show her. She will learn. What else?

I look around me. With just the two of us we manage mostly quite well until visitors descend. That mainly. Maybe the windows. Sometimes ironing. That sort of thing. I turn to his wife: I think once a month for three or four hours would work well. Can we try that for a start?

She nods slowly.

Is all right, he says.

What do you charge? What are your fees?

He is about to answer when she speaks up.

But bathroom? Do you have need for bathroom cleaning?

No, bathrooms I can do myself. Not necessary.

She smiles. Almost.

Then my price is $20 for each one hour. Normally $22, but no bathroom, $20.

The first day she comes, he accompanies her. I leave them with plenty of pots, pans, rags, Brasso and Silvo at the dining room table and they chatter away between them, background to the jumpy rhythm of the computer keys under my fingers. Edward Said would have called the alignment of sound contrapuntal I say to myself and then wonder at the orientalist connections my subconscious has pieced together.

As they leave I attempt to arrange for the following month.

She shakes her head. I will telephone when, she says.

True to her word she calls a few days before the end of the following month.

You want me to come? Again?

Yes, fine.

For the next little while there's silence, a few seconds only perhaps, but long enough for me to take the phone from my ear to look into it and then wonder at myself for a so hopelessly primal an action. Her voice comes back on the line. She clears her throat.

And, Tangea?

Yes?

Eh … I can bring my daughter? Is all right?

She arrives the next day with a child of three, maybe four, a bright-eyed, shy little girl who hides her face in the skirt of her mother's sari. I am just a little dubious. It brings up memories of an amah I had in Hong Kong who similarly asked if she could bring her young son one day. Having been a working mother all my life I am unable to do other than empathise with anyone in this situation, so naturally I had agreed. It had been a particularly torrid day on the magazines – with deadlines on all three editions imminent – and my two-hour commute back from Central to our flat in the New Territories was always a combination of footwork, mini-bus and ferry with all the waiting for connections in between. I had arrived home that day just as she was ready to leave, but she wanted first to show me one of the bedrooms we'd freshly painted the weekend before. It wasn't a good moment standing, tired as I was, in front of that wall which had now been covered, child-high, with crayon. It was a rental apartment; I was horrified and it wasn't until much later I realised that her laughter at my reaction was a sign of her own embarrassment. At the time it made things worse. Later I thought of lots of things I could have done with that wall, including making a feature of the coloured graffiti. But at the time …

Did you bring some toys? I glance now at Shanta's empty hands.

She has her own ways, mutters the mother. Resolutely she moves on past me into the house, the little girl's head turned back towards me as she climbs the stairs clinging to her mother's sari.

I return to my desk, my attention at first fragmented. But the juxtaposition of sound that come from the other room is again quite musical: mother-daughter chatter, the little girl's voice high and ending each time on a question, the mother's a soothing tempo in between.

When I break from my computer for a cup of tea an hour or so later I find she has moved a small rug into the dining room and the child is sitting at her feet amid the gleaming brass.

There's another job that looms and it occurs to me she may want the extra work.

I call the mobile and her husband answers.

I may have some more work for your wife – a one-time job. Could she please call me?

She will call you.

A little while later there's a ring at the door and she stands on the bottom step, her breath coming quickly, as if she has been running.

I explain the job. Cleaning for four hours. A friend's flat in a suburb the other side of the city. I can drive her there and my husband will bring her back. Since it's one-time only, a better rate, say $25 an hour.

Yes, she says. I can do it. Tomorrow? She goes to turn away, looks back over her shoulder and there's that suggestion of a smile again. $25. Very good for me.

When I arrive to pick her up from an address on the edge of the next suburb in a street appropriately enough named Hope Avenue, she emerges with her daughter from the rear of the house.

I can tell she is nervous, that there is a high degree of trust vested in me as she settles the child quickly in the back seat, belts herself in beside me. She stares straight ahead, her hands clasped tightly in her lap.

But before we get to the first roundabout, still staring in front of her, she speaks.

You like Indian food?

Anyone acquainted with me, knows there's no answer to that other than an enthusiastic affirmative.

Your telephone. Not working?

Yes, perfectly fine. I think there's no problem with our phone. Why?

I try to telephone. Many times. Now too late. We have party early this month. But now gone. Good food. Next time please. You, your husband will come

Once I've eased onto the freeway I have a question of my own.

How long have you been here?

She counts on her fingers. Six. Six months.

Do you like it?

Some is good. Other … matters not so …

For the first time she takes her gaze from the road ahead to look sideways out of the passenger window and something tells me that it's not the Swan River she sees swirling past her eyes.

When I leave her at the flat, I suggest she slip the lock on the screen door. She stops me as I step out. Hesitates.

This here … is safe? She glances along the concrete of the corridor and then quickly down at the child.

As I reassure her, I am reminded again how difficult it must be in a country in which you still feel a stranger to get in the car of someone you've met only a couple of times, be driven to the other side of the city and left for four hours in an empty flat with a young child.

She comes to clean another couple of times, calling ahead to confirm the day, bringing the little girl who is still shy, but who still chatters non-stop to her mother and who is still so unspoiled she can sit on a rug playing with bits of paper for hours at a time.

And then I have another idea. For some years now, we've held an annual party which, over time, has turned into a fund-raiser for one dog charity or another. This year we hope it will be bigger than ever and I think for the first time of our getting some help with the food. Next time she arrives, I ask her.

Shanta? Sometime – no hurry for this – can you make some food, just a small amount for my husband and me to try? And then, maybe, later, perhaps a couple of big dishes for a party? Naturally, I pay … you tell me how much.

She beams at me. A full-scale, wide open, gleaming smile that lights up her eyes.

But what? Many dishes to choose. What you want?

I shrug. Chicken, maybe?

She looks quickly sideways, her smile collapsed.

Vegetarian. We are vegetarian. Therefore I can do only …

All right. That's fine.

As she bustles from one job to another that morning why I get the sense that she's planning our menu?

Before she leaves, she comes to me.

After one day, I bring? All right?

No hurry. Whenever. Just a small amount.

But that same evening just as I am finishing off a new *boeuf bourguignon* recipe I'm trying out, the phone rings and it's Shanta.

I can bring the food? In twenty minutes I shall come.

A short while later she bustles up the drive, dressed as if for dinner wearing gold bangles and earrings and a luscious pink sari trimmed with silver thread, holding a plastic ice cream container carefully in front of her. I go to take the food, but she asks to unpack it as she needs the containers, so up the stairs she goes.

She places the container on the central kitchen bench with a small flourish. As she decants the contents into my own bowls, I try to recall just where I've seen that degree of concentrated anticipation before. Although she's totally focused on what she's doing, she's driven by a certain thrill. Of pride in her work, yes. But that's not all. There's something more altogether.

Out on the kitchen counter she sets a glass jar of pickled brinjal; from a margarine container, she deftly decants a potato-and-cauliflower dish I know as *aloo gobi*, but which she calls something else; two different versions of dhal and a double serving of Glad-wrapped chapatti.

She sets it all out quickly, packs up her empty container and the bowls it contained and stands back twisting her open palms one against the other, her eyes glistening into mine.

When I ask her what we owe her, she protests, makes a gesture as if she would pack it all up again, rushes off. The tail of her hot-pink sari streams out behind her as she hurries down the driveway towards her husband's waiting car.

As I watch her go, I remember where I've seen that look before, that look of anticipation, hesitating like water at the rim of a glass too-full. I witnessed it many years ago at a school prize-giving on the open face of a young girl who, as the winners were being announced in the usual suspenseful way, held her hands pressed together under her chin, trying not to breathe so as not to disturb the fragility of the moment, having to hold herself in check, because the fizzing inside her body was not located in her veins or in her brain, but somewhere altogether more central. Because the happiness that just might lie beyond the present hope and fear of it all was beyond the imagining.

I understand then that this food offering is more than a trial run for a party dish, more than a gift, too. It's a symbol of her culture, a statement of identity, the prideful bringing of her home into mine.

I want to join … I want to join, insists Sethe's reincarnated daughter Beloved, from Toni Morrison's book of the same name.

THOUSANDTH MILES

Phuc came to give me flowers and my husband Richard a bottle of wine. He caught two buses and had a fair walk built into his trek from the central city to deliver his gifts. His reason, he said, for coming this evening was because Richard was one of the first people he'd met when he arrived in the country last year. Since then – until Monday of this week when his lease expired and he found a cheaper alternative rental – he had been renting one of our investment units.

'For the future,' he had explained to me on the phone earlier. 'I have to save for future.'

He was a neatly dressed young man who was a lot younger than he had sounded on the phone. Refusing any refreshment other than a glass of water, he sat very erect on our couch, his backpack beside him and his hands tucked tight between his knees. He nodded at Richard. 'Him … he,' he said. 'For me … that man … he something like father.'

At most, my husband would have met with him a couple of times over the year, spoken to him over the phone once, maybe twice. But Richard has that effect on young people.

In a battle to express himself in our language, Phuc explained he was now sharing a house with a group of Vietnamese students. Knowing he was Vietnamese and having enjoyed several weeks in what we perceived as a friendly country a few months before, we were happy for him.

'Ah, much better for you than the flat, I think,' I said. 'Not so lonely.'

He shook his head. 'No,' he said. 'Not like that. Not like that.'

The physical combat might have ended with the capture of Saigon by the North Vietnamese nearly thirty-five years ago, but the hostilities continue. Just the week before, he told us, in his profession as chef he had applied for a job at a Vietnamese restaurant in the city.

'"Where you from?" they ask me. "Vietnam. Just like you," I say. They wave hand. Very angry now. "No, where you from in Vietnam?

Where?" Northern part, I have to say. And so they tell me, "Not wanted here. Go away. Quick, now, go away."'

It was the same, it appeared, with the students in the house he was now sharing. The war between north and south Vietnam may not now be physical, but generations later it clearly continues to fester in the minds and attitudes of both sides. Not only that, but it has spilled over its geographical boundaries, too, something that is relevant here only in that it was a further isolating factor in an already lonely situation.

Phuc stayed for an hour, an hour during which he ventured to the boundary of spoken language in an effort to get us to understand his life story: the poverty of his background, his culinary ambitions and his desire to make good. He came from a small province in the far north of the country and as he talked I couldn't help being reminded of Li Cunxin's powerful autobiography *Mao's Last Dancer*. Even though Cunxin is Chinese and was, at that time, a ballet dancer, there was an uncanny similarity in their stories of striving, persistence and immigration. Phuc's homesickness, one surmised, was not so much for his country as for his wife (who had come out briefly and returned to Vietnam), for his friends and for his mother.

'But my name – Phuc – it mean lucky. Lucky man. I will have luck.'

When Phuc left, Richard drove him to the bus stop. He hadn't touched his drink of water.

When, two days later, we cleaned and readied the flat for the next tenant, I happened to see something written in blue ballpoint pen across the side of a polystyrene plant tub on the small balcony. THOUSANDTH MILES, it read in capital letters. It seemed to me to tell a story of heart-rending homesickness, that phrase that stood between me and a view of the steady stream of people making their way up and down the steep set of steps of the adjoining mountainside three minutes from the Perth city centre.

Turning back into the dim space of the unit, I saw then, clear as he'd been a couple of nights before, Phuc sitting on the single chair in the middle of this one room, a glass of water between his knees, staring out past the carefully blocked words at his view of middle Australia.

ONCE WERE IMMIGRANTS

Once I was a migrant, too, one of many who sailed to Australia in the days of the 'ten-pound passage' on the *Fairsea* in the 1960s. But I had several advantages over Phuc and Shanta. The obvious ones were that I spoke the language, that my skin was white and that my father was Australian.

However, realised only in retrospect, less observable but of no less benefit, was also my lack of roots. If you don't have a sense of home as a place, perhaps it's not quite so difficult to pack up and move on? Or perhaps the tribal instinct, the desire to join, to be a part – for once – of something or somewhere becomes so strong that beside it any disadvantages of a new country are demoted to quibble status? I don't think it's ever easy to make new friends, to start again, but when there's no strong and lasting attachment to the place you've just left – no real familiarity – it certainly removes one difficulty.

In my case, no place had been home for very long; any friends I'd had time to make rapidly became pen-pals. Tea chests and cardboard cartons were a constant in my life from the beginning and my earliest memories are of being the family scribe responsible for the interminable listing of items in each trunk and packing case. At quite a young age, I imagined myself as one of the coloured crystals in a kaleidoscope which, when it was twisted, fell through the air into another space so sometimes I landed upside down surrounded by a totally different set of neighbours, friends and circumstances.

Because I had no real motherland, no geographical place of belonging or familiarity, my immediate family – my mother, father and my sister – were my home. They became the nucleus of my life, a sort of seashell of shelter, so that I became dependent to a greater degree than normal or healthy, I think, on their love and acceptance. As long as I was with them, wherever they moved was home; being removed from this comfort zone as in my several spells at boarding school was a particularly traumatising and disorientating experience.

But unlike me and like Phuc and Shanta, my Aunt Ruby did have roots – a strong comfortable taproot into English soil – where she lived in a small village in Middlesex surrounded by all the other aunts where they'd all, with the exception of my rebel mother, spent most of their lives, and her immigration story is quite different from my own. Several years after their younger son migrated to Perth, they decided to sell up and follow. Why? I often wondered and I asked her once.

Well, dear, I can't say we have very much in common with the others any longer. We're looking for a new life. Different things, you see. We have one son here. And there are your mother and father, of course. We've sold everything back home. A clean break.

One problem they didn't anticipate was that my mother didn't have a great deal in common with Aunt Ruby; an age difference of some thirteen years was one reason, but having seen each other only once in the last thirty was another. A further setback was that their son had been successfully leading his own life for many years and was unlikely to welcome any parental interference in his affairs. But perhaps the most compelling explanation for what went wrong rather quickly lay in her words 'back home'. If there's a place that once was home, how hard must it be to put that behind you? If you have a motherland where family and friends still live, can you ever look back without some degree of longing?

Having never left home, my aunt and uncle were unfamiliar with the notion of homesickness; immigration simply meant replacing the house and goods they'd left behind. So within a short time of landing they had bought a house in the Hills, a new car, furniture, fridge and washer … in short, they replaced everything material they'd had in England. And then they joined the local bridge club, dined regularly with my parents and my parents dined with them. I believe they made a great effort to 'fit in'.

It took eight months, that first time, before they admitted they'd made a mistake. They missed the folks, they said, and Australia wasn't quite right for them. So without more ado, they sold everything they had just bought and went 'back home'.

Imagining everything back in the village to be exactly as they'd left it, they could be forgiven for expecting a warm welcome. But it wasn't to be so easy. Most people's lives –however grand they may appear on the one hand – come down to the minutiae of habit that combine to make up each day and these finer points in the larger picture are quite different for everyone. For one person it might be a daily workout or afternoon tea on Saturdays with the family. For another it might be the daily discussion in the office tearoom of the prior evening's television programme. Or looking forward to the next episode of their favourite sitcom. I remember my first husband John's reaction to the attention span of his family of origin on one of his quick visits 'back home' to England.

They're delighted to see me – for the first ten minutes, that is – and then they go on to talk about their wretched blocked pipes or the price of bread, he ranted. And as for the television! They don't even have the good manners to turn it off; it's flickering away there in the background, turned down low …

The cold reality is that – as delighted as they undoubtedly were to see him and to know he was well and enjoying life – once this was established, he ranked less in importance than the next episode of *When the Boat Comes In*. What appeared incidental to him was part of the warp and weft of their lives.

In the case of my aunt and uncle, the other siblings had been less than happy – openly wounded, you could say – as they struggled to cope with the gap left by their absence, something they privately regarded as desertion. So when Ruby and Ted arrived 'home', there was no prodigal son reception and they had to work hard to try to reinstate the original status quo. But it took only six months this time before they decided they had given up on Australia too easily, and they sold up and returned to Perth where, once again, they bought everything anew.

Sadly, this was to happen a number of times, and with increasing speed, so that in one case their container of household goods was still on its way to England when they were making plans to come back this way. In the end – in this quest to re-join – they spent their savings; my uncle died with the strain of it all and Ruby ended up in a tiny unit in suburban Perth, anonymous and very alone.

When we exchange our homeland or one way of life for another, the transaction is often dominated by one of two contrasting emotions – hopefulness or desperation. However, like many opposites, varying degrees of one tends to exist in the other, and hope and despair are closer cousins than one might think. While my mother's immigration to Australia was accompanied almost entirely by despair, in contrast – in her restless comings and goings – her sister Ruby was propelled by a type of hope that proved just as merciless. It's not just the physical country or house we leave behind, it's the traditions we've learned to take for granted, the familiarity with our surroundings and, above all, the connectedness: the feeling that comes from being part of a tribe that fuelled my mother's despair at her disconnection and Aunt Ruby's attempts to reconnect. At the end of the journey, we open our suitcases and what do we find: hope or despair. Or, as British-Indian novelist Salman Rushdie suggests in *Shame*, is there just an emptiness?

'You can never go back,' they say. But why is this? Is it that we no longer continue to exist for those we've left behind? If they think of us at all, do they remember us as we were when they last saw us, or as we are now: ten, twenty, fifty years later? Memory and Time: those two old crooks and their tricks. What a lot a new country or diaspora has to live up to – and make up for.

Aunt Ruby's immigrant story is as much about loneliness as that of Phuc and Shanta because in the act of leaving her land of origin she ripped out roots she didn't know she had. She was unaware, too, that once she had torn the filaments that held her to home, once she'd left, she could never return because, in the interim, the place itself had changed. She had become as homeless 'back home' as she was in exile. Having established that, she returned to her new country, secure in the knowledge that the bonds of the old no longer existed. That may well have been the case, but bonding in Australia hadn't happened either, so in this extreme case she swung between one state of mind – and being –

and another. And between continents. A pendulum, constantly moving, but going nowhere. Just counting time.

Immigration is not only about quotas or imperial judgements or tightly held opinions as to whether we should or shouldn't accept people from other countries into our own. It's not even necessarily about the geography of being a long way from home. A large part of it is about belonging, the innate human need to be part of a tribe. Another part is about identity, about not losing the bits that make us *us*.

Whether it be through ambition, dislocation, search for self, exile, war or whim, the great majority of us migrated at some time in our histories from west to east or east to west, from one side of the nation to the other or from country to city and back again. Or from one suburb to another which – incidentally – can be just about as unsettling.

It's easy to forget – or not to remember – that we, too, once were immigrants.

The preceding three pieces – "I want to join", "Thousandth Miles" and "Once Were Immigrants" – were published in *Griffith Review* as **Thousandth Miles** and broadcast on *ABC National Radio* as **Once Were Immigrants**.

POSTSCRIPT

As a postscript to this collection, I'm taking the somewhat uncommon step of adding one of my father's short stories. In my family the writing gene was passed down from my grandparents Isidore and Eileen Kozminsky. My grandfather's books are still in print today a century after first publication and my journalist grandmother Eileen wrote for the social magazine *Table Talk* in early twentieth-century Melbourne. The gene – or passion for writing – was carried by my father, passed down to me and onwards to my own daughter Tammy Tansley. Who knows where next it will turn up?

My father, Ken Coton, first became interested in storytelling at Prep School in Melbourne where he conducted lunchtime instalments of improvised serial stories. His first short story was published at age thirteen. As a young man he was a journalist on daily newspapers for some years – an occupation he held responsible for destroying his passion for storytelling, which he called the 'real business of writing'. His favourite author was Paul Gallico whose example 'in telling an emotional story in simple language' he credited with 'rekindling' his desire to write stories once again.

I'm not quite sure when **Then Came Fury** – one of my favourites – was written, but it's set at Epsom Racecourse in Surrey, England, on one of the famous Derby days. Dad – like his father before him – was no gambler, but he loved the tension and excitement of racing and in his London years before and during WWII he would have spent many a meeting at Epsom. However, as the story shows, he was also fully aware of the cruelty of the sport – and in writing about it, did his bit to spread awareness.

The story was first broadcast by the *Australian Broadcasting Commission* around 1970 at a time when I was newly married and living in Dampier in the Northwest of Australia. It was scheduled to be broadcast late one evening and I remember driving to a headland – the best place to get a reception in the Pilbara in those days – to listen to a crackling rendition on the car radio as the sun went down over the Indian Ocean.

It was nearly three decades later that the story was unearthed and re-broadcast by the *British Broadcasting Corporation* which went to some trouble to trace my father for permission.

My father died in 2008 just three weeks short of his 100th birthday. This is for you, Dad.

THEN CAME FURY

by

KEN COTON

The taut ropes of the barrier danced in front of his eyes, a firm breeze ruffled his red hair. Deeply and savagely he inhaled the early summer smell of the emerald turf, backed away nervously as the din of the bustling crowds grew louder – it was a day for memories.

A boy's voice spoke gently to him quietening his excitement and giving Fury that same strange feeling of elation it had so often done before. His ears pricked forward and he stood still, just because that boy had spoken.

They said he was a mad in-bred killer. 'Ten-thousand pounds down the drain. Ought to have known better than to give that kind of money for the son of West Wind and Miracle Lady. Far too closely bred.' That was how his owner Old Man Town reckoned things – and it was a popular reckoning.

But Fury thought differently. He was mettlesome and he could be mad if he wanted to. About as mad as Old Man Town was bad-tempered. It all depended on how one was treated.

The starter was trying to get them into line and Fury was on the outside of eighteen other restless colts. Anyone who was supposed to know anything said it was the best place for a killer and that Old Man Town was lucky to be allowed to race him at all after the last show.

Fury remembered how nearly a year ago that bony horse murderer had tried to bring him home. Scrivens, they called him, a great rider and a jockey you could rely on. Old Man Town and his pool-room friends bet everything on the jockey and Fury started odds-on, the best bet of the year.

Here was the son of a great Derby winner galloping easily at the rear of a tightly-bunched field, ready to slip past whenever he was called upon. Yet Scrivens wasn't satisfied. There was too much at stake and this jockey had his own methods of bringing off a win. Without warning, he brought his whip down two, three times on Fury's rump and dug in the spurs …

Taken by surprise, Fury threw up his head and swung out from his position on the rails putting an end to the racing days of a black filly that happened to be in the way. In an effort to regain control Scrivens swore, raised his whip and spurred him again.

Fighting, frothing, eyes white with rage, Fury had dropped back from the field and was still swinging wide when all of a sudden he changed his tactics. With Scrivens powerless to do more than continue to inflict pain, Fury regained the rails to gallop right through that bunch of two-year-olds as if they were standing still. When he passed the post it was with a length to spare, but without Scrivens. He had brushed that gentleman off on the rails and left him lying on the turf with a compound fracture of his left leg.

It was half an hour before they caught and boxed the newly born terror and when Old Man Town came up and hit him across the nose with his cane, "the killer" – as they were now calling Fury – arranged things so that his mercenary owner would spend a month in bed. But he hadn't meant it that way – he had meant to *kill*.

His reputation as a killer had stuck to him hard; Fury grew to like the great respect these bullies showed and he lived up to his new title pretty well. They turned him out in a huge paddock and let him keep himself in condition, hoping that one day the mad son of West Wind would quieten down and recover some of the money that had "gone down the drain".

His reminiscing ceased abruptly at the sharp cut of a whip nearby as a white colt got slightly out of hand and he made to back through the barrier. That whip was too close for Fury and he chilled inwardly as he got ready to lash out with his great hind legs.

Whips! There would be no more whips for him. He would fight, maim, kill before that happened … He shied from side to side, then that soft firm voice was calling on him again. Small heels, spurless, eased him away quietly.

It was funny, what that boy could do with that red brute, they said in the racecourse bars.

Fury's temper cooled. They were right. He would do anything for this boy they called Mickey. The first person unafraid to walk right up to him. A ragged little stable boy who wanted a job. He'd had a pocket full of sugar too. Fury liked that.

The excitable chestnut danced from side to side as he remembered how he had been ridden since then, bare-backed and bridle-less, right up to Old Man Town. He'd said a bleeding miracle had happened, but it was really just a question of gentleness.

Now Fury turned his gaze away from the still restless and unruly colts and the efforts of their riders to get them in line, to the huge crowd making such a din. He watched the bustle to the vantage points to get the best view and all at once the son of West Wind felt the blood of his sire rise within him. With a toss of his beautiful head, he moved up to the barrier and the starter had his perfect line.

'They're off.'

The cry that went up was followed by a strange silence broken only by thundering hoofs scrambling for position. A grey had jumped away to be almost immediately headed by a big chestnut, just ahead of a small colt which led the rest. Fury was last as they swung around into the mad uphill rush for the mile post.

On they went, the leader now two lengths away from the little black colt, with the white that had caused trouble at the starting post pulling hard into sixth place. At the mile post Mickey urged Fury forward very gently and as they began the curve to Tattenham Corner, he saw the leader four lengths clear of a bay colt that had moved up neatly on the outside. The black was next, then the white, now settling down to the seriousness of the race. Mickey kept hard to the rails, waited for an opening on the inside of a dapple grey as they swung round the Corner. The opening didn't show and he brought Fury around on the outside.

But as he passed a roar went up from the crowd. The jockey on the white had tried to shake up his mount when he accidently flicked Fury with his whip. Wild went Fury as they swung round. That whip again, just as before. His faith gone, he veered across the course and was second last into the straight, paying no heed to the small strong hands that strained to right him. His old mad temper had returned.

'That's the killer,' they would be yelling. 'Up to his old tricks again. He'll kill the boy.'

That boy. Yes! He was clinging to him now, still urging him 'to give it to 'em'. No oaths, no whip, no spurs, just talking to him as he always did. What was he doing to his friend? Fury felt a few pats on his neck, heard the small voice pleading with him.

He straightened up. They wanted a show, did they? Well, he wasn't through yet. The field was nearly a furlong into the straight and the leader was still the big chestnut, but he was being hard ridden and his swishing tail showed he was ready to give in at any moment. He was being strongly challenged by the little black colt and the bay, now neck and neck. The rest of the field was well spread and Fury still had only one behind him. He could sense that even Mickey had given up hope. That would mean everyone counted him out of the running. But they reckoned without the son of West Wind who was just mad enough to think differently.

With head and neck outstretched, his mane flying, he set out after them as if he were stoked by the fires of hell, galloping madly on the trail blazed by his great sire. It all happened just as it had before, but there was purpose and no mad temper in this gallop. Like a flash of red lightning he went through the field, passing one after another until, buoyed up by the excitement of the crowd and the voice of the boy on his back, he burst forth in the glory of that great run.

It was now or never. The big chestnut that had gamely tried to lead all the way gave up as they came out of the dip, leaving the black colt to fight it out with the bay, while a grey a length further back was making what looked like a winning run on the outside. Fury saw it all in a flash as he came up behind them to the gap left between the colt and the rails. The three jockeys saw the danger as he powered up behind them and mercilessly called for one last extra effort from their mounts, but Fury went through the opening with the precision of an arrow, passing them all at the post to win the race of the century.

But as he won, he felt something snap inside him. In a few strides he faltered from a gallop to a walk. The others, pulling up, flashed past and the din grew softer.

He felt the boy jump from his back, his pain dulling as he felt the silk-clad arms wind quickly round his strong neck. His fading vision just managed to take in the anxious freckled tear-wet face. It was a fitting climax that their great Derby would go down in history. Mickey was made. Old Man Town would win, but in winning he would lose. All was well.

Again the pain worried him. For a moment he remembered the green fields of his yearling days as he gambolled with Miracle Lady. He stumbled and fell.

ACKNOWLEDGEMENTS

Firstly, my thanks and deep appreciation to Professor Dennis Haskell for taking the time to read these stories and for his endorsement on the back cover of this edition. Thanks also to my editor Camilla Singh for the splendid job she has done in bringing together this collection from half a world away, to my longtime friend and mentor Athol Barrett whose own generously shared stories sowed the seed for several of these, and to Katrina Tap whose suggestion I write a story based on Ernest Hemingway's famous six-word short story provided the inspiration for **Baby Shoes**. And lastly, my especial thanks to my dear Richard, my daughter Tammy, my son Viv, and my sister Toni for their unwavering support and encouragement. I am immensely grateful to you all.

A number of the pieces have appeared previously, sometimes in different forms: **The Gambler** highly commended in the *FAW Angelo B Natoli National Award,* later published in *Island;* **Middle Man** joint-winner of the *Todhunter Literary Award*; **The Deadly Germ of Doubt** runner-up in a *Qantas* competition; **Endlessly Rocking** was highly commended in the *Julie Lewis National Award,* and later anthologised in *An Alphabetical Amulet*; **The Schoolteacher** was published in *The West Australian Weekend Magazine*; **My Mother Was a Russian Spy** won the *Society of Women Writers' Launceston Tasmania Literary Award*; **What's This Thing Called Sex?** published by *Griffith Review online*; the three pieces "I want to join", "Thousandth miles" and "Once were immigrants" appeared in *Griffith Review* as **Thousandth Miles** and were later broadcast on *ABC National Radio* as **Once Were Immigrants**; Ken Coton's story, **Then Came Fury,** was first broadcast by the *Australian Broadcasting Corporation,* years later by the *British Broadcasting Corporation*.

The extract from J. M. Coetzee's *Summertime* (Vintage) is reprinted with kind permission.

www.ingramcontent.com/pod-product-compliance
Lightning Source LLC
Chambersburg PA
CBHW061016120726
47910CB00006B/1969

* 9 7 8 0 9 9 4 1 6 2 5 4 0 *